The Murder of
Rosa Luxemburg

The Murder of
Rosa Luxemburg

Klaus Gietinger

Translated by Loren Balhorn

VERSO

London • New York

GOETHE INSTITUT

The translation of this work was supported by a grant from the Goethe-Institut which is funded by the German Ministry of Foreign Affairs.

First published in English by Verso 2019
Translation © Loren Balhorn 2018
First published as *Eine Leiche im Landwehrkanal:*
Die Ermordung der Rosa Luxemberg
© Edition Nautilus, 2008

Verso
UK: 6 Meard Street, London W1F 0EG
US: 20 Jay Street, Suite 1010, Brooklyn, NY 11201
versobooks.com

Verso is the imprint of New Left Books

ISBN-13: 978-1-78873-446-2
ISBN-13: 978-1-78873-449-3 (US EBK)
ISBN-13: 978-1-78873-448-6 (UK EBK)

British Library Cataloguing in Publication Data
A catalogue record for this book is available from the British Library

Library of Congress Cataloging-in-Publication Data
A catalog record for this book is available from the Library of Congress

Typeset in Fournier by MJ & N Gavan, Truro, Cornwall
Printed in the UK by CPI Mackays

Contents

Preface to the English Edition   vii

Introduction   1

1. The Shock of Revolt   9
2. The 'Little Napoleon'   13
3. The Arrest   21
4. Eden: The Hotel of No Return   33
5. The Day After   41
6. 'The Strictest Investigation'   49
7. Jorns Is Dragged into the Hunt   55
8. The Trial   67
9. Vogel's Escape and 'Pursuit'   75
10. Passing the Buck   91
11. The Seventh Man   101
12. A Visit from On High   111
13. The Confession   117
14. The Assignment   121
15. Fifty Years Later   123
16. Seventy-Four Years Later   139
17. The Deed and Those Responsible   143

Appendix: Participants in and Supporters of the
  Conspiracy   151
Documents   171

Preface to the English Edition
100 Years of Double Homicide

It was in 1989, just after the Berlin Wall had come down, that I got the crazy idea to make a film about the death of Rosa Luxemburg. Luxemburg was decidedly 'out' at that time – the Soviet Union was falling apart, East Germany had disappeared, and all of a sudden no one with any power or authority in reunified Germany was interested in hearing about Rosa Luxemburg: neither the East German dissidents who had turned Luxemburg's line about the 'freedom of dissenters' against their own allegedly socialist state, nor the West German Social Democrats who had regularly invoked her as sword and shield against the single-party dictatorship that ruled the GDR, the Socialist Unity Party. Rosa Luxemburg was suddenly *persona non grata* in German public life, now viewed primarily as a revolutionary, a woman who advocated revolutionary violence. And in Germany, revolutionary violence is the kind of thing that can get you into trouble – it is something one simply does not do, practically the work of the devil.

I failed to raise any money for my film project. Programming directors at the major German television stations advised me to 'write a family-oriented TV series, or a sitcom' instead. But I continued my research in the footsteps of others before me, such as Heinrich Hannover, Elisabeth Hannover-Drück and Dieter Ertel, and before them Leo Jogiches, Paul Levi and many more. I felt sure that someone would take the work eventually.

Then, before finding an interested publisher, I made a quite unexpected discovery: the collected papers of Waldemar Pabst, the man who boasted to the news magazine *Der Spiegel* in 1962 that he had 'allowed them to be executed'. Housed in the Federal Military Archives in Freiburg, these papers were restricted and thus inaccessible to me. Pabst had not been dead long enough to release them at that point, but someone in the archives must have overlooked this fact, because all of a sudden the relevant files found their way to my desk. I spent weeks sifting through every scrap of paper, uncovering some astonishing information, before turning to other source materials, such as the trial documents from 1919.

The trial for Luxemburg's murder was one of the most laughable travesties of justice in all German history. The murderers' comrades-in-arms presided over the court. Ignoring protests (primarily from Social Democracy's rank-and-file), the government run by the Social Democratic Party (SPD) allowed the double homicide to be covered up and swept under the carpet before the public's very eyes. They had good reason to do so, as I found in my investigation. But it would seem, according to his papers, that Captain Pabst began to spill the beans in his later years (he only died in 1970).

Reprinted several times since first appearing in Germany in 1993, this book has become a minor bestseller of sorts. It was repeatedly attacked by SPD-aligned historians who claimed that Pabst was senile, or had simply lied. True, Pabst never spoke out publicly but rather among comrades – 'between us', as he put it – but that was not what really upset the historians of Social Democracy. Rather, they just could not accept that the things he reported as an eyewitness might be true. What exactly he reported, and more, is laid out in this book.

Ten years ago, the historian with Social Democratic sympathies Hans-Ulrich Wehler had the gall to assert in a radio interview that: 'Whoever unleashes civil war always lives in the shadow of death. If captured by the other side, he will be put up against the wall... Then someone like Noske [the supreme commander of government troops in 1919, a Social Democrat] has to play the bloodhound.'

Today, 100 years after the murder of Rosa Luxemburg (and, lest we forget, Karl Liebknecht), the times seem to be changing once again. At the very least, interest in Rosa Luxemburg appears to be enjoying a revival. As time went by I managed to uncover several new pieces of the puzzle that is this lastingly consequential double homicide.

In closing, I would emphasize the extraordinary fact that, even 100 years after Luxemburg and Liebknecht's murder, the party responsible has yet to admit its culpability. It is high time it did.

Klaus Gietinger
Saarbrucken, Germany
May 2018

Introduction

The murders of Rosa Luxemburg and Karl Liebknecht con-
stitutes one of the great tragedies of the twentieth century.[1]
No other political assassination in German history stirred
public passions and transformed the political climate of the
country like that killing on the night of 15 January 1919, in
front of a hotel with the paradisiacal name of Eden. Their
murders marked the prelude to further political assassinations and a great deal more. As Paul Levi observed, in
his famous plea written three years before the victory of

---

1   Of the same opinion: Ossip K. Flechtheim, *Die KPD in der Weimarer
Republik*, Hamburg: Junius, 1986, 106; Hermann Weber, *Die Wandlung des
deutschen Kommunismus*, Frankfurt: EVA, 1969, 14; Manfred Scharrer, *Die
Spaltung der deutschen Arbeiterbewegung*, Stuttgart: Cordeliers, 1983, 220.
Scharrer would adopt a different position over the course of reunification, and
now portrays himself as one of Luxemburg's sharpest critics, who no longer
finds her murder tragic. Wolf Biermann, happy to quote Luxemburg at the
1976 concert which led to the revocation of his East German citizenship, would
call her into question at the Landwehr Canal in 1999, saying: 'Who knows
whether she would have killed under the tree of freedom' (*Berliner Zeitung*,
14 September 1999), thus indirectly condoning her murder. Similarly denun-
ciatory is Hans Ulrich Wehler, *Deutsche Gesellschaftsgeschichte, 1914–1949*,
Munich: C. H. Beck, 2003, 398 and 537. He repeats the old Social Democratic
legitimizing hypothesis that the murdered had been at fault.

Rosa Luxemburg (1871–1919); Karl Liebknecht (1871–1919)

German fascism, 'here began that unearthly train of the dead, which resumed its course in March 1919 and dragged on for years and years ... murdered and killed'.

Luxemburg and Liebknecht's case epitomized a veritable fall from grace, 'in which murderers went about their work in full knowledge that the courts would fail'.[2] Distortions, obfuscations, aiding and abetting, false accusations and self-incrimination surrounding the deed would follow for years to come. In particular, the trial preceding the court martial of the Garde-Kavallerie-Schützen-Division (the military division to which the perpetrators belonged, hereafter GKSD) – 'a travesty of justice which must be described as one of the greatest legal scandals of our century' – transformed the tragedy into a farce in which quite a few Social Democrats were deeply involved.[3]

---

2 Paul Levi, *Der Jorns-Proʒess*, Berlin: Internationale Verlagsanstalt, 1929, 55.
3 Wolfram Wette, *Gustav Noske*, Düsseldorf: Droste, 1987, 309.

Although one participant's admission of guilt in the 1920s and several trials in the late 1920s and early 1930s would begin to shed some light on the case, these efforts remained hampered by legal wrangling and political setbacks, leading the renowned historian of German Communism, Ossip K. Flechtheim, to conclude resignedly that 'the precise political, moral and legal responsibility of the various protagonists will most likely never be known.'[4]

Yet one of the responsible parties spoke out – at first privately in 1959, then publicly in 1962 – betraying secrets and sparking furious protests with the shamelessness of his admissions, while at the same time earning the approval of some sectors of society, including the West German government of the time. The final act of this tragic comedy began when the historian Joseph Wulf discovered the GKSD court-martial files, along with additional files of the prosecution dating from 1921 to 1925, and provided them to the West German journalist and filmmaker Dieter Ertel.[5]

Ertel not only studied the files, but also interviewed the dubious responsible parties, before turning the affair into a docu-drama which aired exactly fifty years after the murder.[6] These actions promptly got him into trouble, and he would find himself involved in two questionable trials before

---

4   Flechtheim, *KPD in Weimar*, 105.

5   Joseph Wulf (1912–1974), historian and pioneer of Holocaust studies. Around the same time as Wulf, Heinrich Hannover discovered the minutes of the trial and other documents in, among others, the Socialist Unity Party's central party archives. See Elisabeth Hannover-Drück and Heinrich Hannover (eds), *Der Mord an Rosa Luxemburg und Karl Liebknecht. Dokumentation eines politischen Verbrechens*, Frankfurt am Main: Suhrkamp, 1967 (henceforth '*Der Mord*').

6   See documents in the appendix to this volume.

Dieter Ertel was the director of Süddeutscher Rundfunk's documentary film department at the time. Later on, he became the managing director of Südwestfunk
(SWF).

Stuttgart district courts in 1967 and 1970 against the men
he identified as Rosa Luxemburg's assassins. Ertel lost the
case and was forced to retract his accusation. The farce had
reached its final, pathetic climax – a climax only made possible because the Social Democratic government in 1919 had no
interest in revealing the truth behind this crime. The military
court system was in turn able to obfuscate the facts, allowing subsequent lawyers to defer to the seemingly logical and
legal actions of their predecessors in a gigantic monocausal
legalistic chain, stretching on for over fifty years.

In this process, the sham trial before the GKSD court
martial consistently served as the point of departure. For,
according to the logic of subsequent lawyers, nothing that
had been signed and sealed by a German court could pos-
sibly be untrue.

This is why so much confusion continues to reign among
historians even today, as the scholar Ernst Rudolf Huber

knows all too well: 'Even later efforts failed to adequately illuminate the darkness of the circumstances surrounding the deed.'[7]

While Helmut Trotnow's biography of Karl Liebknecht suggests that Otto Runge was the assassin,[8] and Wolfram Wette's biography of Gustav Noske points to First Lieutenant Vogel,[9] whom Hagen Schulze in turn identifies as Liebknecht's murderer,[10] the East German *Illustrierte Geschichte der deutschen Novemberrevolution* (Illustrated History of the German November Revolution) would identify a Vice-Feldwebel Krull as an accomplice as late as 1978,[11] who Jakow Drabkin in turn identifies as the lieutenant on the murder vehicle's footboard.[12] While Leonidas Hill reports that Pflugk-Harttung never stood before a military court[13] and Eberhard Kolb and Reinhard Rürup's compendium of source materials from the Central

---

7   Ernst Rudolf Huber, *Deutsche Verfassungsgeschichte*, Stuttgart, Berlin, Cologne, Mainz: W. Kohlhammer, 1978, vol. 5, 928.

8   Helmut Trotnow, *Karl Liebknecht (1871–1919): A Political Biography*, Hamden, CT: Archon, 1984, 253, n. 294. Trotnow himself appeared confused later on when he, incorrectly reconstructing my work in an essay for a catalogue to an exhibition on Walther Rathenau, cited the autopsy as unreliable, erroneously indicated the time of death and accused a man of the murder who never received this honour (Helmut Trotnow, '…es kam auf einen mehr oder weniger nicht an', in Hans Wilderotter (ed.), *Die Extreme berühren sich – Walter Rathenau 1867–1922*, Berlin: Argon, 1992).

9   Wette, *Noske*, 309, n. 221. Runge is named as the murderer on 866.

10   Hagen Schulze (ed.), *Das Kabinett Scheidemann, 13. Februar bis 20. Juni 1919*, Boppard am Rhein: H. Boldt, 1971, 50.

11   Günter Hortzschansky et al., *Illustrierte Geschichte der deutschen Novemberrevolution*, East Berlin: Dietz, 1978, 313.

12   Jakow S. Drabkin, *Die Novemberrevolution 1918 in Deutschland*, Berlin: DVW, 1968, 518.

13   Leonidas Hill (ed.), *Die Weizsäcker-Papiere 1900–1932*, Frankfurt am Main and Vienna: Proplyäen, 1982, 615, n. 6.

Council[14] introduced a mysterious sailor as the 'alleged' perpetrator, Sibylle Quack concluded in 1983 that to advance any definitive statement on the matter would be 'problematic'.[15]

Alongside the lack of clarity concerning the identities of the perpetrators, rumours have continued to swirl and re-emerge with regularity. Some, for example, claim that leading SPD functionary Philipp Scheidemann placed a bounty on the two socialists' heads,[16] while others assert that fellow leading Communist Wilhelm Pieck, like Judas, betrayed 'Karl and Rosa' on that fateful night.[17] Speculation concerning further potential accomplices also ran wild[18] – and not entirely without justification, as we will see.

That even today's politicians are ill-equipped to confront this generalized confusion was demonstrated when the author of this volume presented his findings at a public event, and was immediately accused by a well-known member of the SPD and veteran of 1968 of peddling a

---

14   Eberhard Kolb (ed.) et al., *Der Zentralrat der Deutschen Sozialistischen Republik, 19.12.1918–8.4.1919. Vom ersten zum zweiten Rätekongreß*, Leiden: Brill, 1968, 678, n. 22; Karl Friedrich Kaul, *Prozesse, die Geschichte machten. Deutscher Pitaval von 1887 bis 1933*, East Berlin: Das Neue Berlin, 1988, 117.

15   Sibylle Quack, *Geistig frei und niemandes Knecht. Paul Levi – Rosa Luxemburg. Politische Arbeit und persönliche Beziehung*, Cologne: Kiepenhauer & Witsch, 1983, 241, n. 10.

16   The accusation that Philipp Scheidemann had posted a bounty was made on the fiftieth anniversary of his death in 1989.

17   The 'traitor' Pieck would be 'captured' in a letter to the editor in the *Süddeutsche Zeitung* on 18 August 1989.

18   One scene co-written by Willi Bredel for the 1953 East German film *Ernst Thälmann: Sohn seiner Klasse* managed to expose the final conspirator in the plot: the American president!

'cock-and-bull story'. Against this confusion, the present volume seeks to clarify specific political, moral and legal responsibilities for the notorious double homicide.[19]

---

19 An important primary source for my research was the papers of Waldemar Pabst, including his unpublished memoirs and countless letters. These files have since been partially digitalized and can be found on the home-page of the Federal Military Archives in Freiburg, at invenio.bundesarchiv. de (last accessed July 2018). I furthermore base myself on conversations conducted by Dieter Ertel with Pabst, before witnesses, in the 1960s. A further tape exists, which former Waffen-SS officer Karl Cerff (then director of the Association of German Engineers in Baden-Württemberg) recorded with Pabst in 1966. Pabst's main papers: Bundesarchiv-Militärarchiv (BA-MA), N 620. Tape recording: BA-MA, N 620/56. Memoir fragment: *Im Kampf gegen die Novemberrevolution*, BA-MA N 620/2. Pabst's additional papers: Stiftung Archiv der Parteien und Massenorganisationen der DDR im Bundesarchiv (BA-SAPMO), NY 4035 (previously NL 35).

1

The Shock of Revolt

The timing and, more than anything, the source of the sailors' uprising in Kiel and other German coastal cities that kicked off the Revolution of 1918–19 took the old rulers by surprise: it was, as one historian would later describe it, 'a spontaneous and elemental revolt from within the armed forces themselves'.[1]

It sent the 'Kaiser's elite', the naval officers who had hitherto regarded themselves as a kind of knightly order of the German Reich, into a state of shock.[2] Martin Niemöller, the anti-Nazi Lutheran pastor, wrote in his autobiography: 'I accepted all the horrors of the war as a matter of course and without being shaken to the depths of my soul ... What did shake my soul to its innermost depths and forced me to

---

1 Ernst-Heinrich Schmidt, *Heimatheer und Revolution*, Stuttgart: DVA, 1981, 42.
2 Heinz Höhne, *Canaris*, trans. J. Maxwell Brownjohn, London: Secker & Warburg, 1979, 12. See also Holger H. Herwig, *The German Naval Officer Corps: A Social and Political History, 1890–1918*, Oxford: Oxford University Press, 1973, 68–101.

Revolutionary sailors in Wilhelmshaven

seek a clear and definite issue for myself was the revolution, which was not merely an upheaval, but a complete breakup. A whole world sank under me at that time.'[3]

After overcoming their initial paralysis, these officers had one thing on their minds: revenge. Revenge for the 'disgrace', the 'humiliation'. They were driven by hatred – a deep hatred for the 'masses', for the revolt, and for those who allegedly fomented it: the Independent Social Democrats (USPD) together with Liebknecht and Luxemburg.[4]

Officers began to organize into brigades. One of the most enterprising figures in this undertaking was a young lieutenant, who appeared to know everything and everyone.

3   Martin Niemöller, *From U-Boat to Pulpit*, trans. Commander D. Hastie Smith, Chicago, IL: Willet, Clark & Co., 1937, 194. See also Herwig, *Officer Corps*, 102–256.

4   Wilfried von Loewenfeld, 'Das Freikorps von Loewenfeld', in Hans Roden (ed.), *Deutsche Soldaten*, Leipzig: Brietkopf & Härtel, 1935, 149ff; Richard Frey, 'Die Versenkung der deutschen Kriegsflotte bei Scapa Flow', in Ernst Jünger (ed.), *Der Kampf um das Reich*, Essen: Kamp, 1929, 52.

Lieutenant Captain Niemöller and his unit in November 1918

So impressed was the Social Democratic official responsible for naval and military affairs, Gustav Noske (see the portrait in the appendix, 155), that he made him his liaison officer in Kiel, and thus into a pivotal element of the counterrevolution. The man's name was Wilhelm Canaris (see portrait on 151).

He preferred working in the background, in the shadows. 'Canaris ... was fascinated by these cat-and-mouse games with the enemy ... As one who had experimented with invisible inks and assumed false names in his boyhood, he was fond of the mysterious – of veiled allusions and the concealment of ulterior motives and intentions.'[5] He also believed that the sailors had been manipulated, that the 'Marxist-Communist foe had surreptitiously infiltrated the fleet and subverted it with the aid of undercover accomplices on board.'[6]

---

5   Höhne, *Canaris*, 20.
6   Ibid., 51.

A friend of Canaris's established a relatively small naval officers' association. These officers were 'shock troops',[7] forming in a capital city swept up by 'the red flood' around the turn of 1918–19.[8] They were housed at In den Zelten, no. 4, from where they were 'called on for special operations'.[9]

The name of their leader was Lieutenant Commander ('Kaleu') Horst von Pflugk-Harttung (see portrait on 161). He and his naval squadron were in turn under the command of a division which would play a decisive role in the 'battle for the Reich'. In fact, they were led by a captain whom Canaris also knew very well: Waldemar Pabst, the first general staff officer of the Garde-Kavallerie-Schützen-Division.

---

7   *Darstellungen aus den Nachkriegskämpfen deutscher Truppen und Freikorps. Band 6: Die Wirren in der Reichshauptstadt und im nördlichen Deutschland 1918–1920* (henceforth '*Wirren*', Berlin: Mittler, 1940, 53; Hans von Kessel, *Handgranaten und rote Fahnen*, Berlin: Verlag für Kulturpolitik, 1933, 163.

8   Hessisches Hauptstaatsarchiv Wiesbaden (HStA), *Spruchkammerakten Heinrich Stiege*, Abt. 520 F/A 409-499, 18. The exact name of this 'special unit' of Kaleu von Pflugk-Harttung was '*Marineoffiziers Eskadron beim 5. Ulanenregiment*', *Wirren*,183 and 185.

9   Landesarchiv Berlin (LAB), Re 58, no. 464, Akten des Landgerichts II, Berlin, 'Strafsache gegen Hermann W. Souchon', vol. 1, 2.

2

The 'Little Napoleon'

Originally an elite unit of the Kaiser under the command of Lieutenant General Heinrich von Hofmann, the GKSD had been deployed to the Western Front in 1918.[1] But since von Hofmann suffered from a heart ailment, the unit was soon commanded by Pabst, who joined the GKSD in March 1918 on General Erich Ludendorff's orders.[2] Short, vain, ambitious and thirsty for power, Pabst would become one of the most notorious figures of the 1918–19 revolution. His influence and above all his position of strength within the military have tended to be underestimated in the past.[3]

With the GKSD, the 'remarkable'[4] Pabst held sway over the strongest counterrevolutionary military formation –

---

1 Huber, *Verfassungsgeschichte*, 901, n. 34.

2 See document III in the appendix to this volume.

3 Klaus Gietinger, *Der Konterrevolutionär. Waldemar Pabst – eine deutsche Karriere*, Hamburg: Nautilus, 2009.

4 Hagen Schulze, *Freikorps und Republik*. Boppard am Rhein: Boldt, 1969, 29, n. 125.

Soldiers of the Garde-Kavallerie-Schützen-Division [GKSD] in Berlin, January 1919.

the 'backbone of all deployed troops'[5] upon which Noske's authority was based.[6]

As soon as news of the revolution reached him, Pabst began driving the GKSD 'home in forced marches', fully intent on sweeping away 'the rule of the inferior'.[7] Pabst and the GKSD reached Potsdam's Wildpark train station on 30 November 1918.

Captain Waldemar Pabst in 1914

---

5   *Wirren*, 36; see also the table on 182ff.

6   BA-SAPMO, NY 4056/7 (previously NL 56/7), 11–13, letter from Noske to the Austrian chancellor dated 10 October 1928.

7   Waldemar Pabst, 'Spartakus', in Kurt Hotzel (ed.), *Deutscher Aufstand*, Stuttgart: Kohlhammer, 1934, 28. On the return march see also Pabst, *Memoirs*, 3ff.

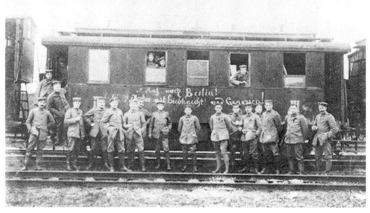

Graffiti on the train car reads 'Off to Berlin! Down with Liebknecht and comrades!'

Here, Pabst experienced his first encounter with 'Red Berlin'. Volksbeauftragte or 'People's Deputy' Emil Barth, a member of the newly-formed revolutionary government, had been expecting him.

> BARTH: Hey, you, come over here!
>
> PABST: Hey, you, come over here!
>
> BARTH: I am your superior!
>
> PABST: Have you lost your mind?

As soon as Barth introduced Pabst to his companions, including the 'Councillor of Deserters', Pabst lost his composure. Pabst: 'Clear the train platform in three minutes, or expect a thrashing!'[8]

---

8 See document II in the appendix to this volume; see also Pabst, *Memoirs*, 12–15 and 22–4; Emil Barth, *Aus der Werkstatt der Revolution*, Berlin: Hoffmann, 1919, 75; *Wirren*, 32. The interpretation of the meeting found in Ulrich Kluge, *Soldatenräte und Revolution*, Göttingen: Vandenhoeck & Ruprecht, 1975, 443, n. 171 is incorrect.

The GKSD set up its headquarters in Nikolassee, near Berlin's Wannsee, and 'agreed as a precaution that no unbidden guests would be permitted'.[9] Shortly thereafter, on 10 December 1918, Pabst marched his GKSD into Berlin through the city's iconic Brandenburg Gate.

Emil Barth

Nevertheless, the attempted putsch against the Workers' and Soldiers' Councils, plotted by the Supreme Army Command (Oberste Heeresleitung, OHL) with SPD leader Friedrich Ebert's knowledge, would fail.[10]

The old social order's gleaming defences were falling apart, and Berlin appeared to be in the hands of the masses. Pabst single-handedly held the GKSD together, at least to some extent,[11] insulating them from all external influences and imparting continuous 'educational' instruction that reflected his reactionary worldview.

Thanks to this, the GKSD would be one of the few combat-ready units left over from the old armed forces. On 24 December 1918, Pabst led the attack on the revolutionary Volksmarinedivision, or 'People's Naval Division', as

---

9   See document III in the appendix to this volume.

10   Kluge, *Soldatenräte*, 233ff.

11   Pabst, *Memoirs*, 28f. See also the transcript of a secret meeting of the OHL on 26 December 1919 in Heinz Hürten (ed.), *Zwischen Revolution und Kapp-Putsch. Militär und Innenpolitik 1918–1920*, Düsseldorf: Droste, 1977, 32f. The officer mistakenly identified as 'v. Pape' is actually Pabst.

Friedrich Ebert

ordered by Ebert,[12] not hesitating to use gas grenades in his artillery strikes.[13]

Yet the thundering of the artillery did not fade away unheard. 'Counterrevolution by the officers!' was the echo it called forth. It flew from mouth to mouth, was taken up by the factory sirens and stirred up the farthest corners of the sea of buildings that was Berlin, and the dragon seed that had been sown over the previous weeks rose up prodigiously ... in frantic rage, the unleashed mutiny leapt ... at our troops.[14]

---

12   Susanne Miller (ed.), *Die Regierung der Volksbeauftragten 1918/19*, 2 vols, Düsseldorf: Droste, 1969, nos 70–72, 77, 78; BA-MA, NL 620/2, report by Pabst dated 25 December 1918.

13   Rudolf Rotheit, who was no friend of the sailors, later wrote: 'The green-yellow traces of gas grenades could be seen here for a long time afterwards, although subsequently it was denied that such grenades had been fired.' Rudolf Rotheit, *Das Berliner Schloß im Zeichen der Novemberrevolution*, Berlin: Scherl, 1923, 88. The cannon that fired on the castle carried the – historically ironic – inscription '*Ultima ratio regis*' ('The king's final argument').

14   Pabst, 'Spartakus', 34f.

The Berlin City Palace destroyed by the GKSD on Ebert's orders.

The masses forced an end to the operation.[15]

Pabst had now witnessed the power of the masses at first hand, along with its demoralizing effect on the institution that was the very essence of his life: the Army. Rosa Luxemburg's 'dragon seed' had arisen. Germany no longer had a royal army. Nevertheless, Pabst refused to give up. He retreated to the edge of Berlin with what remained of his

15   *Wirren*, 42.

'Summarily executed' 'Spartacists'. Noske would write in 1933: 'And I cleared away the scum and cleaned up as fast as was possible at the time.'

troops, dismissed the elements 'infested with Spartacism' and recruited volunteers to develop a powerful squadron that would be as motivated as he was himself. Disguised as a civilian, he attended gatherings where Liebknecht spoke, and soon identified him as his most fearsome adversary.[16]

He became fully convinced of the 'danger' represented by the Spartacists when one of his own officers asked him to allow Rosa Luxemburg to address the brigade. The officer, 'a Catholic nobleman', had heard Luxemburg speak and 'believed her to be a saint, a new Messiah', with an incredible sense of purpose.[17] Pabst later recalled: 'At that moment I completely understood the danger Frau Luxemburg posed. She was more dangerous than all the others, even

16 Pabst, *Memoirs*, 66.
17 See document I in the appendix to this volume.

those bearing arms.' He decided to eliminate her. The outbreak of the January Uprising provided the necessary opportunity.[18]

Pabst offered Noske his services in the Luisenstift boarding school located in Berlin's Dahlem neighbourhood, which had been appropriated for military purposes, and soon became 'one of the most enterprising' assistants,[19] eager to wipe out the 'rabble-rousers' once and for all.

Gustav Noske inspects the troops of the anti-republican Loewenfeld naval officers' brigade.

---

18   That this uprising came at the 'right time' for the Freikorps and the gigantic military apparatus gathered in Berlin's suburbs is also evidenced by the disappointment of 'the troops' at the weak defence put up by 'Spartacus'. See *Wirren*, 73.

19   Gustav Noske, *Von Kiel bis Kapp. Zur Geschichte der deutschen Revolution*, Berlin: Verlag für Politik und Wirtschaft, 1920, 72.

3

The Arrest

In the early morning of 15 January 1919, with all strategically significant points in Berlin long secured by the right-wing paramilitaries known as Freikorps, the resistance of the insurgents crushed, and the first 'shootings of fugitives' already underway, the GKSD set up its new headquarters in the luxurious Hotel Eden, erected in 1912.[1]

The hotel nevertheless continued to house civilian guests, such as the former Chancellor of the Reich, Bernhard von Bülow. Pabst's GKSD was not only paid by the Supreme Army Command,[2] but also received direct financial support from two German industrialists, Hugo Stinnes and Friedrich Minoux.[3]

---

1 Pabst, *Memoirs*, 64. The Hotel Eden was located at the three-way intersection of Kurfürstendamm (today's Budapester Straße), Kurfürstenstraße and Nürnberger Straße, directly across from Berlin Zoo. It was destroyed in the Second World War and never rebuilt. The Hotel Eden's construction plans can be found in LAB, Rep. 202, nos 4835–40.

2 Interview with Pabst, *Der Spiegel* 16, 1962, 38.

3 Pabst, *Memoirs*, 30. Hugo Stinnes (1870–1924), industry magnate. Friedrich Minoux (1877–1945), industrialist and for a while owner of the so-called Wannsee Villa that hosted the Wannsee Conference in 1942.

The Hotel Eden stood directly opposite the entrance to the Berlin Zoological Garden.

Pabst cultivated excellent relations with Berlin's Reichs-bürgerrat (Council of Reich Citizens, a counterrevolutionary alliance of middle-class politicians and businessmen), and particularly with its chairman, the banker and millionaire Salomon Marx.[4] After all, Pabst also had ties to Eduard Stadtler, chairman of the Anti-Bolshevik League, which was in turn generously funded by big industry.[5]

At this point in time, the GKSD also held command over the Reinhard Regiment, the Pflugk-Harttung naval

4   Salomon Marx, banker (1866–1936), founder of the reactionary Citizens' Council of Greater Berlin in 1918 and its national confederation, the Council of Reich Citizens. He served as executive director of the Norddeutsche Elektrizitäts und Stahlwerke, leading member of the vehemently national-ist Deutschnationale Volkspartei, owner of the Internationale Handelsbank KGaA Berlin, chairman of the board of Carl Lindström AG, Berliner AG für Eisengießerei und Maschinenfabrikationen, and the Portland-Cementwerk Schwanebeck AG.

5   Eduard Stadtler, *Als Antibolschewist 1918/19*, Düsseldorf: Neuer Zeitverlag, 1936, 48.

squadron, and the so-called Einwohnerwehren, or Citizens' Defence, all of which were founded with the shared aim of defeating the revolution.[6]

Pabst himself had played a significant role in the formation of these units.[7] As early as their time in Dahlem, Noske had ordered Lieutenant Friedrich W. von Oertzen to tap Liebknecht's telephone.[8] In parallel, both Noske and Pabst monitored

Crude propaganda against Luxemburg and Liebknecht (their names are written on the cartoons' loincloths)

Liebknecht's written correspondence.[9]

Gang-like organizations and civil defence units hunted for Liebknecht and Luxemburg throughout the city. Whether such actions were legal did not seem to worry anyone.[10]

---

6   See the tables in *Wirren*, 183ff.

7   Letter from Pabst to Ertel dated 3 March 1967, *Dokumentation der Vor- und Nachgeschichte des Verfahrens Souchon gegen SDR/Bausch/Ertel (1966–1975) im Archiv des SDR* (henceforth *Dokumentation SDR*), 110. See also BA-MA, PH 8V/27.

8   Friedrich W. von Oertzen, *Die deutschen Freikorps*, Munich: Bruckmann, 1936, 284.

9   BA-Berlin, Reichspostministerium 47.01, no. 4818, 326.

10   Liebknecht, Luxemburg and Paul Levi had already received death threats in December 1918 from a unit of the 'Social Democratic' Reichstag Regiment under the command of the mentally disturbed building director, Hasso von Tyszka. The Spartacus leaders were later 'freed' by a unit of the Sicherheitswehr Eichhorn under the direction of a dubious character in the revolution named Prinz. Erich Prinz, a 'painter', later claimed that Scheidemann and Georg Sklarz had placed a bounty of 100,000 marks on

Numerous espionage units from 'pro-government associations' worked themselves into a frenzied state of activity,
sometimes in competition with one another.[11] The most
important of these were the 'Espionage Departments' of
Pabst's GKSD,[12] the commandant's office run by Anton
Fischer,[13] and the Reichstag Regiment.[14]

---

the heads of Liebknecht and Luxemburg. The signatures on this 'document',
however, were forged by Prinz himself, who had the document prepared by
his girlfriend Hilde Plaumann – she would later kill herself with cocaine.

Scheidemann never signed such a bounty note, nor did he ever give any
corresponding verbal 'orders'. However, Scheidemann's son-in-law Fritz
Henck, co-founder of the Reichstag Regiment which was generously funded
by the Council of Reich Citizens, frequently claimed that this order had
existed. Scheidemann, 'who was also too smart to do such a thing' (Pabst),
was subjected to such accusations for decades as a result of his suspicious
son-in-law's 'military work'. Scheidemann himself would face personal consequences from the SPD leadership's lack of interest in forming genuinely
republican military units: they instead preferred to work with the anti-
democratic military, and even set up reactionary associations financed by the
big bourgeoisie from within 'their own ranks'.

The forged document: LAB, Rep. 58, no. 2072, vol. 1, 8a. The sentence
from the Scheidemann/Prinz case: LAB, Rep. 58, no. 2072, vol. 3, 150–77.
On Hilde Plaumann's suicide: LAB, Rep. 58, no. 2072, vol. 3, 145.

11   Richard Müller, *Der Bürgerkrieg in Deutschland*, Berlin: Olle &
Wolter, 1974 [1925], 171.

12   BA-MA, PH 8V/vol. 22, 7; Pabst's letter to Ertel dated 16 January
1967: *Dokumentation SDR*, 101; Kessel, *Handgranaten*, 222; Wilhelm
Reinhard, *1918/19. Die Wehen der Republik*, Berlin: Brunnen, 1933, 77.

13   Anton Fischer, SPD, served as city commandant from 23 December
1918 to 7 January 1919. His extremely dubious role during this period
remains virtually unresearched to this day, and offers a wide field of study
to social democratic historians. The following has been proven: Fischer,
like the GKSD, received support from the Council of Reich Citizens run by
the banker Marx, who sat on the advisory committee of the commandant's
office, which in turn was stationed in the Crown Prince's Palace on Unter
den Linden in central Berlin. A spy was generously rewarded by Fischer
with fifteen marks per day, plus expenses, and 200 to 300 marks per useful
discovery. More information on the financial and hierarchical relations
of the commandant's office can be found in a lawyer's inventory from the
Scheidemann/Prinz trial: LAB, Rep. 58, no. 2072, vol. 3, 57–75.

14   On this see BA-Koblenz, R 32 I 1239, as well as LAB, Rep. 58, no.

These espionage organizations had connections to the state prosecutors Robert Weismann[15] and Karl Zumbroich.[16] Pabst claims not to have known the precise location of Luxemburg and Liebknecht when the brigade moved from Dahlem to the Hotel Eden,[17] but had received tips that they were located somewhere in the western part of Berlin.[18]

On the evening of 15 January 1919, five members of the counterrevolutionary Wilmersdorfer Bürgerwehr,

---

408–410, 433. Despite what its name might suggest, the Reichstag Regiment was by no means a republican regiment. That Social Democrats held positions of command was not enough to make it such. It was a Freikorps unit packed with reactionary, anti-democratic elements and financed by the Sklarz brothers, two war profiteers.

15   See LAB, Rep. 58, no. 6021. Dr Robert Weismann's presence as a public prosecutor lent all of the arrest actions undertaken by Fischer's commandant's office the appearance of legality. He also disposed of excellent contacts in the GKSD. Weismann was the investigating official against Karl Radek in February 1919. He served as the Prussian State Commissioner for Public Order from 1920 to 1923. In 1927 he was accused of being involved in a bribery scandal. In 1928 he became state secretary in Prussia and Otto Braun's right-hand man. In 1933 the Nazis castigated him as a traitor to the German people, and he emigrated the same year. He died in New York in 1942.

16   Weismann's colleague Karl Zumbroich (dates of birth and death unknown) later served as a public prosecutor in the trial of Georg Ledebour (USPD) for the latter's participation in the January Uprising. Although keen to convict the defendant, Zumbroich maintained that the January Uprising had not constituted high treason, and Ledebour was acquitted. Zumbroich was involved in the cover-up of the murder of thirty sailors by First Lieutenant Marloh in March 1919. He committed high treason himself when he agreed to be appointed minister of justice during the Kapp Putsch in 1920.

17   The most important of Pabst's espionage organizations was the so-called '*fliegende Kraftfahrstaffel Kessel*', established in January 1919 and assigned to Pabst in March. Men recruited from this group included Ernst Tamschick (who murdered Leo Jogiches), Heinrich Dorrenbach, as well as the killer of the thirty sailors, Otto Marloh. The men of the squadron formed the basis of the Security Police (the Sicherheitspolizei, or 'SiPo') which Pabst consolidated together with the support of Noske and the Social Democratic Prussian Minister of Justice Wolfgang Heine (1861–1944), and from which many Nazi Party members later emerged.

18   See document III in the appendix to this volume.

another reactionary citizens' militia, walked into the bar on the corner of Mannheimer Straße and Berliner Straße, adjoining the building at Mannheimer Straße 43.

The five men were the merchant Bruno Lindner, the distiller Wilhelm Moering, and three other uniformed citizens, named Jurczck (also a merchant), Schwarz and Jantz.[19] In

Dr Robert Weismann
(1869–1942)

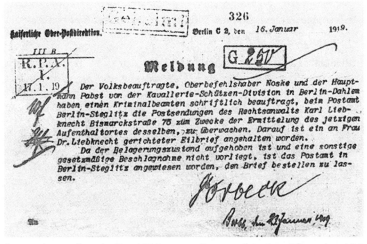

Secret telegram from the Royal (!) Executive Director of the Post Office, dated 16 January 1919: 'The People's Deputy, Commander-in-Chief Noske and Captain Pabst of the Kavallerie-Schützen-Division in Berlin-Dahlem ordered a detective in writing to monitor the letters of lawyer Karl Liebknecht, Bismarckstraße 75, in order to find out his current location.'

---

19   The following information is found in the report by public prosecutor Ortmann (henceforth 'Ortmann's report') to Prussian Minister of Justice Heine dated 5 February and 24 February 1919, BA-Berlin, *Nachlass Heine*,

the bar, they asked the bartender about the apartment of a certain Marcusson, located in the next-door building.[20] There, they would later indicate, they expected to find a Spartacist meeting place and arms, although in reality they were searching for Liebknecht and Luxemburg.[21] The source of the tip-off remains unknown to this day. Without a warrant of any kind, they forced their way into the apartment.[22]

They stopped a gentleman located in the room who sought to flee upon their arrival, and searched him for his papers. In doing so, they found a residency permit in Liebknecht's name and his photograph. Because he called himself Marcusson but this did not appear believable to them, Lindner and Moering then took him in the car to headquarters in the Cecilienschule in order to determine his identity.[23]

nos 144, 3–7 and 10–14: the Bürgerwehr was founded on 10 January 1919. Its 'superior department' was the GKSD. Because the government of the People's Deputies had neglected – against all SPD party congress resolutions – to abolish the military court system after the revolution of 9 November 1918, only the Bürgerwehr members were interrogated about the events of 15 January. The main participants in that fateful night were military men and thus enjoyed the protection of the military court system. Public Prosecutor Ortmann even investigated Moering and Lindner on charges of unlawful detention, but the proceedings came to nothing (as was to be expected).

20 See Frau Marcusson's testimony, BA-MA, PH 8V/vol. 6, 28. Siegfried Marcusson was a businessman and a member of the USPD as well as the Workers' and Soldiers' Council in Wilmersdorf, a suburb of Berlin. His wife Wanda was a friend of Rosa Luxemburg's.

21 BA-MA, PH 8V/vol. 13, 214, Lindner's testimony.

22 Ortmann's report, 10.

23 Ortmann's report, 3. The school is located on Nikolsburger Platz. See the 11 January 1919 issue of the *Berliner-Börsen-Courier*; Heinz Knobloch, *Meine liebste Mathilde*, East Berlin: Der Morgen, 1985, 132; BA-MA, PH 8/27, 1.

Left: the building at Mannheimer Straße 43 on the day after Luxemburg and Liebknecht's 'arrest', with the Wilmersdorf Bürgerwehr posing in front of it and Wilhelm Moering and Bruno Lindner (both wearing hats) in the middle. Right: the same building today.

The automobile was driven by a man named Güttinger, and the front-seat passenger was named Probst. While Liebknecht was driven to the Cecilienschule, Jurczck, Schwartz and Jantz remained in the apartment to conduct 'further assessments'. A woman who 'appeared suspicious' – none other than Rosa Luxemburg herself – was placed under arrest.[24]

A man who entered the house around 21:00, claiming he wanted to bring Liebknecht and Luxemburg forged identification papers, was 'arrested and searched by the soldiers upon entering the apartment'. The man was Wilhelm Pieck, a leading member of the Communist Party of Germany, or KPD.[25]

---

24   BA-MA, PH 8V/vol. 13, 211, Lindner's testimony. Lindner would testify in May 1919 during the murder trial: 'Fräulein Luxemburg said she was not Fräulein Luxemburg, but Frau Luxemburg.'

25   Wilhelm Pieck in Isle Schiel (ed.), *Karl und Rosa: Erinnerungen*, East Berlin: Dietz, 1971, 194f.

Also involved in the arrest of Luxemburg and Pieck was a certain Sebelin who, according to his own account, had contacted the relevant police station (No. 8 Berlin-Schöneberg) before Luxemburg's arrest and received two uniformed police officers to assist him. Around the same time, a strange phone call from the Cecilienschule informed the Reich Chancellery

Wilhelm Pieck (1876–1960)

of Liebknecht's arrest. The call was answered by the Chancellery's deputy press officer, Robert Breuer.[26]

Left: Ulrich Rauscher (1884–1930), journalist, served as the government's press officer in 1919–1920, member of the SPD. According to Pabst, he was an alcoholic. Right: Otto Landsberg (1869–1957), SPD member, lawyer and People's Deputy. He served as Minister of Justice in 1919.

---

26 Breuer was 'coincidentally' a member of the Wilmersdorf branch of the SPD at the same time.

By his own account, Breuer informed the caller, Bürger-wehr member Pollmann, that without a warrant the arrest was illegal, yet he also claimed to have forwarded the message to 'the department responsible'.[27] It remains unclear which individual Breuer meant, whether his superior Ulrich Rauscher or perhaps People's Deputy Otto Landsberg. That the department concerned did not respond to the message was explained by Breuer with the circumstance 'that in those days the wildest rumours were dispatched to us from non-responsible departments, partic-ularly news of arrests'.[28]

However, the chairman of the Wilmersdorf Citizens' Council, Fabian, claimed that the intent and purpose of Pollmann's phone call to the Reich Chancellery had been to find out what should be done with Liebknecht. Breuer had answered that he would receive instructions in five minutes. Allegedly, the Bürgerwehr waited for a response for half an hour, in vain.[29]

Thus, Güttinger, Probst, Lindner and Moering trans-ported Liebknecht from the Cecilienschule to the Hotel Eden at around 21:30, delivering him to the 'senior

---

27   BA-Koblenz, R 43 I 2676, 10, report by Breuer dated 2 April 1919, also housed in BA-Berlin, *Mikrofilm Reichskanzlei* 19190 (this microfilm is identical to BA-Koblenz, R 43 I 2676).

28   Ortmann's report, 4. Pieck's arrest is not mentioned in public prose-cutor Ortmann's hearings. The members of the Bürgerwehr kept it a secret. Pieck was only mentioned in the trial as 'editor Dr Schröder from the *Rote Fahne*', BA-MA, PH 8V/vol. 13, 201. This fed rumours of his possible activ-ity as a spy. Yet Pabst certainly would have revealed such a fact, just as he 'exposed' Pieck's willingness to talk that night, claiming he revealed details about the Spartacus League's alleged military build-up. Pabst never spoke of Pieck being involved in espionage, however.

29   BA-Koblenz, R 43 I 2676, 6f, report by state prosecutor Hagemann.

authority', the GKSD. From there, the four drove back to Mannheimer Straße and picked up Luxemburg and Pieck. Both were likewise taken to the Hotel Eden, around 22:00.

Pabst later claimed to have first learned of the Spartacus leaders' arrest when they were 'delivered free of charge, so to speak'.[30] Citizens' Council chairman Fabian awarded everyone involved in the arrest the sum of 1,700 marks, an enormous amount of money at the time.[31]

The eight Bürgerwehr men involved (including three businessmen) received a total of 13,600 marks as their bounty. The Wilmersdorf Citizens' Council was a sub-department of the Council of Reich Citizens led by the banker Marx, the originator of this 'support for the middle classes'. Bruno Lindner, the leader of the courageous businessmen, would later receive even more money for his prowess.

The Reich Treasury, on the other hand, proved less successful in matters of finance. On the day of the double homicide, this institution had launched a search for the fabled riches of the 'Bolshevists' and instructed the Deutsche Bank – contrary to standard practice – to provide information on monies from 'leaders of the Spartacus group', 'in order to secure the claims of the German Reich against Russia'. Yet the Deutsche Bank was unable to deliver, despite directing other banks to join the search in the name of the Treasury. Only a few hundred marks were found in the accounts of Karl Liebknecht's brother Theodor and that of the socialist leader's wife.

---

30   See document III in the appendix to this volume.
31   Ortmann's report, 4.

It was thus impossible to take back the millions which the Supreme Army Command had gleefully pumped into the Bolshevik revolution and reroute them into the monetary circuits of the German counterrevolution. One bank director, somewhat insulted, responded: 'To my knowledge, we do not count any Spartacists among our customers.'[32]

---

32   BA-Berlin, 80 Ba2/Deutsche Bank, Rechtsabteilung, vol. 372, 1–21.

4
Eden: The Hotel of No Return

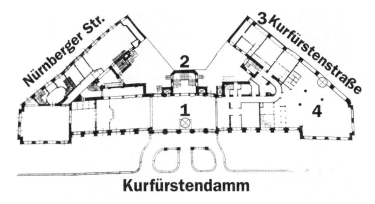

Construction plans for the Hotel Eden, ground floor. The revolving doors (1) facing the Kurfürstendamm (known today as Budapester Straße) and the stairwell (2) are clearly visible. On the upper right is the side entrance from Kurfürstenstraße (3). The café in the bottom right corner (4) served as a guard room.

Karl Liebknecht was led through the main entrance and lobby and up to the first floor of the Hotel Eden at around 21:30.

Pabst had installed his headquarters here across two spacious rooms, the 'Little Hall', the former casino, and the

'Little Salon', where he carried out his duties.[1] Liebknecht was led into the Little Salon and presented to Captain Pabst.[2]

The news that the Spartacus leader had arrived created a pogrom-like mood among the hotel's guests and the officers and men of the GKSD who were there.

According to the highly vivid account given by the murderers' defence lawyer, Fritz Grünspach, a kind of excitement broke out that he called 'German fever', as quoted in *Republik*, a left-wing magazine of the time.[3]

A collective thrill quivered through the luxury hotel. Liebknecht, fully aware of what lay before him, continued to identify himself to Pabst as Marcusson, but was betrayed by the initials on his clothing.[4] Pabst moved to the Little Hall next door and engaged in consultations with his adjutant, Captain von Pflugk-Harttung; his deputy, Captain Rühle von Lilienstern, was probably also present.

It was decided to summon the naval squadron of Captain Lieutenant Pflugk-Harttung from its quarters on In den Zelten Street, in aid of Liebknecht's further 'treatment'.[5] The captain drove there in an open NSU, the same automobile in which Liebknecht would later be taken away,

---

1   BA-MA, PH 8V/vol. 12, 48 and. vol. 15, 764, Pflugk-Harttung's testimonies; vol. 12, 129, Liepmann's testimony.

2   BA-MA, PH 8V/vol. 13, 193, Pabst's testimony.

3   BA-MA, PH 8V/vol. 17, 990, Grünspach's statement. The lawyer Dr Grünspach defended all of the accused in the 1919 trial, and represented Pabst during his prosecution following the Kapp Putsch in 1920. The lawyer also gave Runge 3,000 marks as bribe money in 1920. He died in the 1920s. Pabst stated in his 1966 interview with former SS officer Cerff: 'You won't like what I'm about to tell you, the defence counsel was a Jew.'

4   See document I in the appendix to this volume.

5   PH 8V/vol. 12, 194, Pabst's testimony.

and returned with his brother and four young officers. These were First Naval Lieutenant Ulrich von Ritgen, Naval Lieutenant Heinrich Stiege, Naval Lieutenant Bruno Schulze, and Naval Lieutenant Hermann W. Souchon (see the appendix, p. 151). All of them were veritable giants, measuring up to 1.90 metres.

These 'shock troops' in military uniform arrived at the Hotel Eden around 21:45.[6] Liebknecht was taken out of the Little Salon by these men at around 22:45. A brief and intense political debate had allegedly taken place shortly beforehand.[7] Liebknecht was then led down the steps to the hotel's side exit, while guests and men in uniform shouted insults and spat at him.[8]

An advertisement for the Assault Battalion Schmidt, which belonged to the GKSD and was stationed in Zossen, and housed a man who belonged to Pabst's special commando unit the night of the murder: Hermann W. Souchon. Luxemburg's corpse was transported to his location on Noske's orders.

Soldiers lined the streets[9] in front of the hotel, which was securely cordoned off.[10] Liebknecht and his guards stepped

---

6   *Wirren*, 53 and 73.

7   BA-MA, PH 8V/vol. 12, 50, Pflugk-Harttung's testimony. The precise times can only be deduced from Jorns's 'pre-investigation', and the testimony given in the trial, with great difficulty, whereas the indications given by civilians are more credible.

8   See the construction plans for the Hotel Eden.

9   BA-MA, PH 8V/vol. 1, 109, letter from engineer Otto Wiener.

10   BA-MA, PH 8V/vol. 13, 330, the waiter Krupp's testimony.

into the car.[11] Liebknecht sat in the back; Stiege was next to him, Kaleu Pflugk-Harttung in front of him, next to the driver, Peschel. Schulze stood on the right footboard, infantryman Friedrich on the left.

Lieutenant Liepmann (see portrait on 154),[12] also an aide-de-camp to Pabst but not one of the naval officers, boarded the car as well. He regarded himself as the leader of the transport, since everyone but him was wearing squad coats, but was disabused of that notion by Pflugk-Harttung.[13] Another uniformed man, infantryman Runge (see portrait on 164), who stood guard inside the front entrance to the right of the revolving door, also felt duped – for one Captain Petri,[14] unaware of the 'decisions' reached above him on the first floor, had bribed Runge out of fear that Liebknecht would leave the hotel alive.[15]

Runge watched through the glass of the revolving door as Liebknecht was led through the side exit. He ran around the Hotel Eden together with the chauffeur Güttinger, reaching the automobile just as Liebknecht sat down between the two disguised officers. Runge struck him with the butt

11   According to the officers' testimony, BA-MA, PH 8V/vol. 12, 46ff, 92ff, 101ff, 116ff, 122ff, 143ff.

12   See also Hermann Simon, 'Bemerkungen zu Rudolf Liepmann, einem Beteiligten an der Ermordung von Karl Liebknecht', in Helge Grabitz, Klaus Bästlein and Johannes Tuchel (eds), *Die Normalität des Verbrechens. Bilanz und Perspektiven der Forschung zu nationalsozialistischen Gewaltverbrechen*, Berlin: Hentrich, 1994.

13   Liepmann's testimony in the first Jorns trial, as reported by the *Vossische Zeitung* on 21 April 1929; BA-MA, PH 8V/vol. 12, 56, Pflugk-Harttung's testimony.

14   Petri was Pabst's railway officer and later committed suicide, Oertzen, *Freikorps*, 502, n. 87.

15   Pabst, *Memoirs*, 68. See document II in the appendix to this volume, as well as Pabst's taped interview.

of his rifle. Hit hard, Liebknecht instinctively ducked the second blow. As he did so, blood sprayed onto Stiege's trousers. Liebknecht cried: 'I'm bleeding!' The automobile started up.

Albrecht Freiherr von Wechmar explains to the actor playing infantryman Runge, Friedrich G. Beckhaus, how to act fifty years after the murder.

A man wearing a sailor's cap and a pilot's jacket, von Rzewuski, jumped onto the automobile, punched Liebknecht in the face with his fist, and jumped back off. The officers only thought to take Liebknecht to the first-aid station after he had been murdered and they returned from the Tiergarten.

Entrance to the Zoological Garden today. The first-aid station was located here in 1919.

Shortly after 22:00, Rosa Luxemburg and Wilhelm Pieck arrived at the hotel and were led through the lobby, mobbed by frenzied hotel guests and uniformed men —Luxemburg was insulted as a 'whore' — and brought to the first floor. Pieck was made to wait in a cramped nook between the rooms, under heavy guard, while Rosa Luxemburg was presented to Pabst in the Little Hall. At this time, Liebknecht was still next door in the Salon.

Pabst recalls their encounter: 'Are you Frau Luxemburg?' In response, she said: Please decide for yourself. Then I said, according to this picture it must be you. To this she countered: If you say so! I thus knew just as much as I had beforehand.'[16] Shortly thereafter – Liebknecht had just been ushered out of the Little Salon – she was most likely brought in through the side door to that room. In front of Pabst, whose office it was, she mended the hem of her skirt which had been damaged during the journey[17] and read a bit of Goethe's *Faust*.[18]

Liebknecht was left at the first-aid station near the Berlin Zoo, as an unidentified dead body, at 23:15. The naval officers drove back to the hotel and delivered their report to Pabst in the Little Hall. Rosa Luxemburg was taken away at around 23:40. Retired First Lieutenant Vogel (see portrait on 169), who had been appointed to lead the transport, picked her up and led her through the lobby to the main entrance.

As he had with Liebknecht (and again unbeknownst to Pabst), Runge lay in wait, determined to earn Captain Petri's promised reward. He had even refused the change of guard at 23:00.[19] Vogel let Luxemburg walk ahead of him through the propped-open revolving doors. Runge struck her violently with the butt of his rifle. Knocked unconscious, she fell backwards, losing a shoe[20] and her handbag. The soldier Kurt Becker took it as a trophy. One of the guarding officers, Albrecht Freiherr von Wechmar (later a military advisor on Dieter Ertel's television film about the murder),

16   BA-MA, PH 8V/vol. 13, 195, also printed in *Der Mord*, 67.

17   Pabst, 'Spartacus', 38.

18   Personal message from Günther Nollau. See also *Der Spiegel* (1), 1970, 49 as well as *Dokumentation SDR*, 429.

19   *Die Freiheit* 54, 28 February 1920, Franz Flick's testimony.

20   BA-MA, PH 8V/vol. 15, 760, testimony by Kohler the elevator attendant; 778, testimony by the laundress Anna Wandinger.

The map shows the path along which the Hotel Eden murderers escorted their victims.

stole out of the same bag a letter from Clara Zetkin, which he would sell to the historian Hermann Weber for several hundred marks in 1969.

Lying on the ground, Luxemburg received a second blow from Runge. Only then did Vogel feel obliged to 'intervene'. She was dragged to the car, 'hauled in' and thrown onto the back seat as 'blood streamed from her nose and mouth'.[21]

Infantryman Max Weber sat down to her left, while to her right sat infantryman Willy Grantke. Infantryman Hermann Poppe stood on the left footboard.[22] The driver,

---

21   BA-MA, PH 8V/vol. 13, 329, Pauline Baumgärtner's testimony.
22   The following is according to the testimony of the accompanying soldiers, PH 8V/vol. 14, 571ff, vol. 16, 609ff, 680ff. Max Weber (1893–?)

Hermann Janschkow, sat in front (the steering wheel was on the right side), and the front-seat passenger and co-driver was Richard Hall. Vogel also boarded the car. As the open-topped Priamus rolled down the driveway, von Rzewuski again leaped forward and punched the unconscious Luxemburg twice in the face, before jumping off. The automobile headed towards the Cornelius Bridge. At the level of Nürnberger Straße, roughly forty metres from the hotel entrance, a shot was fired at close range, which 'entered on the left side before the ear and exited on the other side slightly lower down', leading to a 'separation of the base of the skull' and a 'severing of the lower jaw'.[23]

Rosa Luxemburg was killed instantly. It was 23:45 on 15 January 1919.

---

lived in the Berlin neighbourhood of Friedrichshain after the Second World War and was evidently subjected to a renewed interrogation by the East German Ministry for State Security in the 1960s about the events surrounding 15 January 1919; Federal Commissioner for the Records of the State Security Service of the former German Democratic Republic (BStU), MfS HA IX/11 AS 6/69, vol. 7, 69f. Willy Grantke (1900–1972) also lived in East Germany after the war, and faced difficulties due to his participation in the Luxemburg transport (according to information provided by Rainer Raddatz). No further biographical details are known of Hermann Poppe (1899–?), despite searches during the trial of Souchon vs. Dieter Ertel and the SDR in 1969.

23   BA-MA, PH 8V/vol. 6, 43, Privy Medical Councillor Dr Strassmann's autopsy findings. Strassmann took the liberty of noting that it 'appears on the whole rather curious that a shot was fired under these circumstances, which after all entailed a significant danger to the transport soldiers as well'.

5

The Day After

Around 03:00 that same night, Pabst woke his commander, Lieutenant General von Hofmann, and gave him a truthful account of what had occurred. Hofmann, who would later serve as a judge in the murder trial, remarked that he certainly would not have given such an order, but quickly promised Pabst his backing and assumed 'responsibility'.[1]

Pabst's telephone would not cease to ring in the hours to come. He informed his commanding department, led by von Lüttwitz, that Liebknecht had been shot

Kurt von Schleicher (1882–1934), served as a major in the general staff of the OHL in 1919. In 1932 he served as the last Chancellor of the Reich before Adolf Hitler. He was killed by an assassination squad during the Night of the Long Knives in 1934.

---

1   The following is according to Pabst, *Memoirs*, 70ff as well as Pabst's taped interview. See also documents I and II in the appendix to this volume.

while attempting to escape and Luxemburg had been killed by the mob. Captain von Schleicher, who received the call, congratulated Pabst on the action.

Pabst, however, defended himself against von Schleicher's 'assumptions'. Receiving a call from Rauscher around 06:00 ordering him to appear at the Reich Chancellery in the morning, in order to deliver his report, Pabst refused. Von Schleicher called back minutes later and again ordered Pabst to come to the Chancellery, on Field Marshall Paul von Hindenburg's authority. At the same time, he gave Pabst some personal advice: to prepare for the consequences and initiate proceedings against himself. Pabst thus had no choice but to make his way to the Reich Chancellery. He recalls a discussion with the People's Deputies in the Reich Chancellery on the morning of 16 January.[2] That it took place was confirmed by Kriegsgerichtsrat (court martial councillor) Kurtzig in the first Jorns trial.[3] As he himself tells it, Pabst was well-equipped for the encounter. He first placed the GKSD on alert, and then, accompanied by multiple heavily-armed trucks and fifty of his best men (including the murderers), rode to Wilhelmstraße. He gave the order to occupy the Reich Chancellery should he or his commander, von Hofmann, not exit the building by a certain hour. It would not have been a problem for Pabst to occupy the Chancellery, as the guard unit at the time was comprised of the anti-republican 'Suppe Troop', on the

---

2   Pabst incorrectly indicates 17 January in his *Memoirs*, 70.

3   Kurtzig's testimony in the first Jorns trial as reported in the *Berliner Tageblatt* on 20 April 1929. See also Levi, *Jorns-Proʒess*, 24. Kurtzig's testimony in the second Jorns trial is more detailed: see *Vorwärts*, 31 January 1930.

Guardsmen in the garden of the Reich Chancellery in Wilhelmstraße

People's Deputies' orders and under the command of the Reinhard Regiment, which in turn belonged to the GKSD.

Besides the People's Deputies, General von Lüttwitz, Lieutenant General von Hofmann and Kriegsgerichtsrat Kurtzig also participated in the meeting at the Reich Chancellery.[4]

Pabst described the session as follows: Landsberg was the official most sharply opposed to him, demanding immediate arrests. Ebert and Noske were more moderate, and both shook his hand. To avoid the foreseeable storm of public outrage, it was ultimately agreed to initiate investigatory proceedings, albeit by the division's own military

---

4 No minutes of the meeting exist. According to Pabst and Kurtzig, it took place shortly after 08:00. The government's shared meeting with the Central Council took place at 13:00, according to the WTB (Wolffsches Telegrafenbüro), this time without the military. See Kolb and Rürup, *Zentralrat*, no. 55. Walter Oehme (*Damals in der Reichskanzlei*, East Berlin: Kongress, 1958, 312ff) does not mention it at all, although his report only begins at 09:00.

court. The SPD leadership had once again demonstrated its 'insouciance' vis-à-vis the old military apparatus.

This insouciance would later be depicted, and not only by Pabst, as outright friendliness. It seemed that the leadership had also forgotten about the demand for independent courts, that had been confirmed by every previous SPD party congress. They affably agreed to allow the murderers' own comrades to preside over their trial, as the Council of People's Deputies (comprised of SPD and USPD) had failed to do away with 'all of the nonsense of the military tribunals' back in November 1918.[5] It appears downright grotesque when Kurtzig, who was initially tasked with the investigation, later reports that von Hofmann had been the one to suggest that members of the Executive Council and the Central Council also participate in the investigation.[6]

Pabst could most certainly be satisfied as he left the Chancellery together with his two superiors, von Hofmann and von Lüttwitz. Von Hofmann ordered a court-martial investigation to be opened that same day,[7] and allowed von Lüttwitz to arrest the transport leader, First Lieutenant Vogel, 'because sufficient suspicion exists that the necessary measures to protect the detainees were lacking'.[8] A government proclamation issued on the same day promised 'the strictest investigation' and, should protocols have been

---

5   See *Volksstimme Magdeburg*, 16 May 1919. Scheidemann would state in December 1918: 'The foolish pranks of certain officers are child's play compared to the shenanigans of the Bolshevist buffoons.'

6   See n. 3 <c5>.

7   BA-MA, PH 8V/vol. 1, 4.

8   BA-MA, PH 8V/vol. 1, 90.

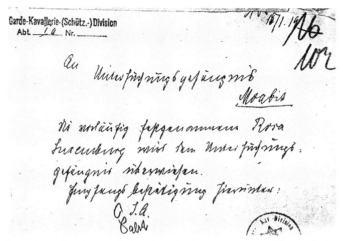

Rosa Luxemburg's 'transfer' to the Moabit prison, signed by Wilhelm Pabst. The spoken orders he gave were, of course, different.

violated, to respond 'with the utmost severity.'[9] Around the same time, the Berlin press began reporting the death of the Spartacus leaders in the terms of an announcement by the Wolffsche Telegrafenbüro (WTB), a leading wire service. The WTB's report was practically identical to the 'official account' by GKSD propaganda boss, Dr Fritz Grabowsky, who had prepared the report the very same night. The Eden's manager, Herr Ott, read the report aloud to hotel staff on the morning of 16 January, remarking: 'That is how it was.'[10]

Grabowsky had excellent connections to the WTB, thanks to which he had been able to spread false news,

---

9   Hermann Müller, *Die Novemberrevolution*, Berlin: Bücherkreis, 1928, 272.

10   BA-MA, PH 8V/vol. 13, 334f., vol. 15, 796; Ortmann's report, 3. Charges against hotel manager Ott for perjury were later filed by the public prosecutor, yet proceedings were eventually dropped, as ever in the Luxemburg/Liebknecht case.

rumours and, when it suited Pabst's interests, a pogrom-like atmosphere on numerous occasions already. The 'official account' went as follows.[11]

After his brief interrogation at the Hotel Eden, Liebknecht was due to be taken to Moabit prison.[12] But news of his arrest had spread, and a mass of people had gathered outside the hotel. Some had managed to force their way into the hotel atrium. For this reason, Liebknecht was hustled out through the side entrance on Kurfürstenstraße, but a crowd had gathered there as well. Cutting a path through the crush had proven difficult. After Liebknecht sat down in the open-topped car, people pressed forward and began hitting him. The vehicle quickly drove off towards Moabit through the Tiergarten, but was forced to halt near the Neuer See due to engine trouble. They then continued with Liebknecht on foot. He tore free and ran, ignoring several warnings, and was shot dead by the military escort.

The mob outside the hotel appeared even more hostile to Frau Luxemburg as she was led through the main entrance. The escort soon found itself in the midst of an 'agitated throng', as the crowd 'began striking Rosa Luxemburg'.[13] She was hurried into the automobile. They were about to drive off when 'a man emerged from the crowd, jumped onto the footboard and fired a shot at Frau Luxemburg from a pistol'. The car was then stopped in front of the canal by

---

11   BA-MA, PH 8V/vol. 1, 1ff, also reprinted in *Der Mord*, 36–9.

12   See also Pabst's 'official' order, BA-MA, PH 8V/vol. 1, 102.

13   On the topos of the 'threatening mob' in Freikorps literature, see Klaus Theleweit, *Männerphantasien*, 2 vols, Basel and Frankfurt am Main: Roter Stern, 1977, vol. 2, 10–109.

The Lichtenstein Bridge over the Landwehr Canal, circa 1925.

another crowd of people, who wrestled Frau Luxemburg's body away from the escort. This utterly implausible abduction was invented because Vogel had thrown the corpse into the Landwehr Canal (one of the many waterways running through Berlin), against Pabst's orders.[14]

---

14   Handwritten note by Pabst on Hans Beuthner's sworn affidavit from 19 December 1968, BA-MA, N 620/46. See also document I in the appendix to this volume.

6

'The Strictest Investigation'

Days later, substantial doubts began to emerge with regard to Grabowsky's story. Eye-witness accounts agreed that no civilians, even less a large crowd, had been present in front of the Hotel Eden at the time in question, as the building had already been cordoned off.[1] Court martial officer Kurtzig of the GKSD, obviously doing his best to conduct an honest investigation,[2] had interrogated the leader of Liebknecht's transport, Kaleu von Pflugk-Harttung, on the evening of 16 January and had him arrested the same night.[3] Kurtzig would later state that he was deeply concerned that the officers were indeed guilty of a major crime.

But Kurtzig was then assigned another court martial officer, 'for support', one who had earned his spurs in China

---

1   BA-MA, PH 8V/vol. 1, 109, letter from Otto Wiener; 139, letter from Sergeant Alker. See also *Die Freiheit*, 17 January 1919.

2   Former people's deputy Hugo Haase declared his faith in him in the *Vorwärts* on 18 January 1919.

3   BA-MA, PH 8V/vol. 1, 13a R. See also the *Berliner Tageblatt*, 20 April 1929; *Vorwärts*, 30 January 1930.

and the 'German South West' and was now to investigate the Luxemburg case: Kriegsgerichtsrat Paul Jorns (see portrait on 153).

Jorns soon persuaded Judge von Hofmann to relieve Kurtzig and allow him to investigate both cases alone.[4] The man behind this manoeuvre was in fact Pabst himself, for whom the rebellious court-martial officer was simply too decent.[5] Jorns's first move was to release the two prime suspects,

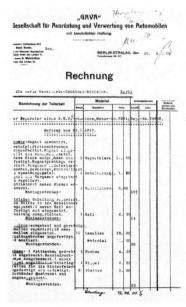

The bill for repairs (!) to the NSU automobile used to transport Liebknecht.

Vogel and von Pflugk-Harttung, despite the risk of evidence being tampered with.[6] The NSU, the vehicle which had supposedly broken down in the Tiergarten, was only turned over to an officer for 'evaluation' six days after the incident.[7]

The Priamus, the car in which Luxemburg had ridden, was not examined at all. The leaders of the investigation became the targets of intense public scrutiny from the

---

4   Hofmann's letter to the Reich government on 21 January 1919, BA-Berlin, *Akten der Reichskanzlei (RK)* no. 2494/15, 6.

5   See document I in the appendix to this volume.

6   BA-MA, PH 8V/vol. 1, 90/90R; Levi, *Jorns-Prozess*, 8 and 26.

7   BA-MA, PH 8V/vol. 14, 464, testimony by 'expert' Lieutenant Herbst; BA-MA, PH 8V/vol. 5, 18f.

beginning. The socialist paper *Die Freiheit* in particular (the Communist Party's *Rote Fahne* was banned at the time), echoing the Executive Council of the Workers' and Soldiers' Councils of Greater Berlin, as well as the SPD's Central Council of the Socialist Republic, expressed grave doubts concerning the court's impartiality. Resolutions of protest passed by workers' assemblies began to mount. Calls for an independent court and even a special commission grew louder.[8]

In formal legal terms, the government could have tasked a civil court with the investigation. But the People's Deputies from the SPD continued to profess absolute trust in 'their' military. The justification for this attitude is worth quoting: 'As nothing is to be changed concerning the appointed court's responsibility as defined by the military criminal court law, no one will be denied his legal judge.'[9] The last half-sentence would show up with almost the exact same wording in article 105 of the Weimar constitution, drafted that same year. A letter written by the government

8   Telegram of protest sent by Karl's brother, Theodor Liebknecht, on 17 January 1919, BA Berlin, RK no. 2494/14, 14. Richard Müller (USPD) called for a special commission in the name of the Executive Council. Such commissions were not uncommon (similar to modern-day parliamentary investigatory subcommittees), yet the motion was ignored by the SPD government. See Richard Müller's letter to the government dated 22 January 1919, 30. See also *Die Freiheit*, 17–24 January 1919. The Central Council passed a motion calling for the trial to be transferred to a civil court on 28 February 29; see Kolb and Rürup, *Zentralrat*, no. 90, 92 and 94. See also Gerhard Engel et al. (eds), *Groß-Berliner Arbeiter- und Soldatenräte in der Revolution 1918/19*, vol. 2, Berlin: De Gruyter, 1997, docs 28, 32, 33, 35, 51 and 60.

9   Letter from the SPD People's Deputies government to the Executive Council, BA-Berlin, RK no. 2494/14. Letter dated 27 January 1919, 23. See also Landsberg's excuses in his testimony in the first Jorns trial, as reported in the *Berliner Tageblatt* on 18 April 1929.

to SPD members in the town of Emden speaks of 'utterly objective jurists', claiming it was 'self-evident that all certifiably guilty persons would be punished with the utmost severity'.[10]

The SPD People's Deputies' sole concession was to accept observers from the Executive and Central Councils, as suggested by von Hofmann.[11]

Jorns made these men's job as difficult as possible, at first not permitting them to question witnesses at all, and later only after a cumbersome procedure. The observers' suggestions were ignored, while their proposed cross-examinations of important witnesses either did not occur or were long delayed. Motions to arrest suspects were dismissed. The observers had scant confidence in Jorns's method of conducting interrogations.[12]

Despite a 'promptly launched manhunt', Kriegsgerichtsrat Jorns failed to apprehend infantryman Otto Wilhelm Runge, who had severely injured both victims with the butt of his rifle. This was because every one of Jorns's decrees and letters was sent through the headquarters of the GKSD. Jorns had even set himself up as Pabst's neighbour in the

---

10   Letter from the SPD People's Deputies government to the Emden SPD dated 27 January 1919, BA-Berlin, *Akten der Reichskanzlei betreffend Aufklärung der Umstände unter denen Dr. Karl Liebknecht starb*, no. 2494/14. 23. See also BStU, MfS, HA IX/11, AS 6/69, vol. 15, 30.

11   Oskar Rusch (1884–1935), SPD and Paul Wegmann (1980–1945), USPD were members of the Greater Berlin Workers' and Soldiers' Council. For more on them see also the introduction to Kolb and Rurüp, *Zentralrat*. On the observers' work see also BA-MA, PH 8V/vol. 1, 26f, 56, 59, 78, 91, 172ff, vol. 2, 4, 23ff, 66, 92, 94, vol. 4, 101, vol. 5, 31, 42.

12   Struve's and Wegmann's testimony in the first Jorns trial, as reported in the *Frankfurter Zeitung* and *Berliner Tageblatt* on 21 April 1929.

The 'Central Council of the German Socialist Republic'. Hugo Struve (1890–?), SPD (no. 1 in the photo), and Hermann Wäger (1883–1942), SPD (no. 14), also served as civilian observers.

Hotel Eden for this purpose (on the second floor, above the café). It was one of the prime suspects, Captain von Pflugk-Harttung, who processed these decrees. They were then sent to Pabst's desk before being forwarded to the government, the ministry of war or other departments.[13]

---

13   *Berliner Tageblatt*, 26 May 1929; Levi, *Jorns-Prozess*, 40.

7
Jorns Is Dragged into the Hunt

A letter from the former people's deputy Hugo Haase would soon help Jorns move things along.[1]

Haase declared that Rosa Luxemburg's corpse had been thrown into the Landwehr Canal by men in uniform, and named the guards stationed on the Lichtenstein Bridge who had observed this action. Jorns continued to delay. Attempting to conceal the fact that Vogel had permitted Luxemburg's corpse to be disposed of in this fashion, Jorns falsified testimony and changed 'a quarter of an hour' to 'twenty-four hours' in a report to the government.[2]

The investigation probably would have petered out at this point and a proper court trial never would have taken place, were it not for an article written by the Marxist revolutionary Leo Jogiches in the *Rote Fahne* on 12 February 1919, which reconstructed the events with uncanny veracity and

---

1 BA-MA, PH 8V/vol. 1, 161–4, dated 23 January 1919. Partially reprinted in *Der Mord*, 50. Hugo Haase was assassinated in 1919.

2 See BA-MA, PH 8V/vol. 1, 133R and 187; Levi, *Jorns-Prozess*, 10.

Rosa!","Fasst an!","Raus damit!", aus dem Wagen ge-
davongeschleppt worden seit hat sich bisher völlige
klärung nicht schaffen lassen. Der Nachtportier des
Schmidt hat angegeben: Der Posten, der Frau Luxemburg
versetzt habe, habe ihm 24 Stunden später gesagt:"Die
t, die schwimmt schon längst! Wir sind nicht weit ge-
t!" Schmidt will den Mann eine Weile nicht auf seinem
dem Portal gesehen aber auch nicht besonders auf ihn
ben, und kann andererseits auch nicht sagen, ob der

The original and Jorns's forgery. Jorns would excuse his forging of files ten years later as a mistake made by the person taking minutes. The minutes taker was also blamed for additional 'discrepancies'.

sparked further public outrage. Jogiches's article identified Pflugk-Harttung and his companions as Karl Liebknecht's murderers, Vogel as Rosa Luxemburg's murderer, and Pabst as the man behind the operation.

As Jorns continued to fail to conduct arrests, the GKSD announced through Grabowsky and the WTB that the

Die Rote Fahne

Zentralorgan der Kommunistischen Partei Deutschlands (Spartakusbund)

Nr. 26 — Mittwoch, 12. Februar 1919 — Preis 10 Pfg.

Der Mord an Liebknecht und Luxemburg

Die Tat und die Täter

Leo Jogiches's article in the *Rote Fahne* on 12 February 1919. Leo Jogiches, the author, was 'shot while trying to escape' in police custody in March 1919.

Rote Fahne was simply summarizing the results of its investigation,[3] while a consultation of the observers with the Reich government in Weimar produced no concrete results. When Noske, Landsberg and Scheidemann continued to defend the obviously biased military court against their own comrades, the observers resigned their posts and published a sharply-worded resolution:

---

3 BA-MA, PH 8V/vol. 1, 46.

The outraged sense of justice has remained silent for far too long. All overt and secret obstacles standing in the way of revealing the truth must now be done away with. As the government evidently possesses neither the strength nor the will to facilitate the breakthrough of justice, we appeal to the public to remove all of the obstacles, particularly the entire military court system, through powerful pressure on the government. A privileged special court cannot be allowed to persist as a backdrop to conceal the most atrocious crime. The German people in their totality are responsible before the world and history for pillorying and bringing to justice those guilty of the murder of comrades Liebknecht and Luxemburg.[4]

The Prussian minister of justice, Wolfgang Heine (SPD), felt compelled to defend the military court system against the accusations of his party colleagues Struve and former colleagues Rusch and Wegmann in the pages of the *Vorwärts*.[5] And yet he did not entirely believe his own claims, for on the same day he demanded a new report

---

4   Signed by Rusch, Wegmann and Struve. The complete text can be found in *Die Freiheit* and *Republik*, 16 February 1919 as well as in Kolb and Rürup, *Zentralrat*, no. 89. BA-Koblenz, *Handakte Wäger* 454-3, 30. See the verdict of the Stuttgart district court dated 12 February 1970, 33; verdict of the Stuttgart superior district court dated 20 January 1971, 77, *Dokumentation SDR*, 977 and 1408. Hermann Wäger would remain as the lone observer, believing that leaving the trial would 'achieve nothing'. His decision to remain, however, was used by the judges of the district court in 1970–71, as well as the superior district court, as evidence that Jorns's investigations were conducted properly. This was precisely the situation his colleagues had sought to avoid.

5   *Vorwärts*, 18 February 1919. Wolfgang Heine (1861–1944), SPD, Prussian Minister of Justice and the Interior. Together with Pabst, he initiated the establishment of the military Security Police (SiPo) against the majority of the Schutzpolizei, or 'Uniformed Police'.

from state prosecutor Ortmann[6] (acting against the civilians involved in the murder), and complained in a letter to Landsberg, Noske and the Ministry of War on 19 February about the way in which Jorns was handling the investigation.[7] Someone else was also unsettled by the *Rote Fahne* article: city councillor Grützner,[8] who had taken over the guard in the Hotel Eden café one day after the murder, contacted Jorns. He reported being asked by a lieutenant – citing Pabst's authority – to convince the guards to 'testify favourably about the incident with Rosa Luxemburg'.[9]

This constituted the first concrete evidence that the real mastermind was Pabst. As a result, it seems Jorns seriously considered arresting Pabst, probably in view of protecting his own reputation, and called on Judge von Hofmann to do so. When von Hofmann refused, Jorns overcame his scruples and continued to allow his decrees to be sent across Pabst's desk.[10]

Vogel admitted to throwing Rosa Luxemburg in the Landwehr Canal on 18 February, but 'no arrest was made' and Vogel was 'enjoined ... not to speak of their interrogation' with the drivers Janschkow and Hall.[11] Vogel's arrest would only occur on 20 February, as a result of pressure from Heine, 'for violating his obligations as leader of

---

6   Ortmann's report, 10: 'Auftrag vom 17. Februar 1919'.

7   Partially reprinted in *Vossische Zeitung*, 18 April 1929.

8   See Paul Levi, 'Der Verdacht Pabst', *Arbeiter-Zeitung* 136, 17 May 1929. Grützner later became the governor of Merseburg and joined the SPD. The *Rote Fahne* would claim he switched over to the Nazi Party in 1931.

9   BA-MA, PH 8V/vol. 1, 40–4.

10   See also the correspondence between Pabst and Ertel dated 16 and 19 December 1967, *Dokumentation SDR*, 155–8.

11   BA-MA, PH 8V/vol. 1, 83, Jorns's note dated 18 February 1919.

the transport'.[12] Meanwhile, the ongoing public protests were making People's Deputy Landsberg feel increasingly uncomfortable. Although he defended the military tribunal in the *Vorwärts*, even after the observers had withdrawn,[13] he now summoned Jorns to meet him in Weimar. He flew into a fit of rage when Jorns presented the meagre results of the investigation behind the stage of the National Theatre.[14] Landsberg calmed down, however, when Jorns (who had kept silent regarding the investigation's most important findings[15]) promised to arrest von Pflugk-Harttung and the officers involved in Liebknecht's shooting. He would only do so eight days later. Pabst would later explain why: he was getting married on 28 February, and his commander, von Hofmann, had promised not to detain anyone from the Liebknecht transport commando until after the event. During the heavily guarded celebration, the newlyweds received a telegram of congratulations from Noske. 'The groom read the telegram aloud and gloated: He's already learning some manners. Well, have we not raised him right?' Pabst would write to Noske the same day to deny that the alleged statement had been uttered: 'I remain, Herr Minister, your utterly loyal W. Pabst.'[16]

---

12   Heine's testimony in the second Jorns trial, reported in *Vorwärts* 57, 7 February 1930.

13   *Vorwärts* 49, 20 February 1919.

14   Landsberg's testimony in the first Jorns trial, as reported in the *Berliner Tageblatt*, 18 April 1929.

15   See the exchange of words between Levi, Landsberg and Jorns in the first Jorns trial as reported in the *Berliner Tageblatt*, 18 April 1929.

16   Pabst, *Memoirs*, 74. The arrest warrants were in fact first issued on 28 February 1919; see BA-MA, PH 8V/vol. 2, 174; BA-SAPMO, NY 4056/3 (previously NL 56/3), 5. On the wedding, see *Die Freiheit*, 18 March 1919; as well as a letter from Pabst to Noske, in which he denies the quote printed

However, shortly before his arrest, Jorns's investigation landed on the desk of Captain von Pflugk-Harttung.
After Runge, who 'ended up' on the Danish border under
the name of 'Orderly Dünnwald' at Pabst's urging,[17]
was finally captured in April 1919 thanks to a tip-off from
another unit, Jorns first held a 'private' conversation with
him. When Runge told him he had received money, the
investigating magistrate responded: 'Well, don't you see,
you have nothing to fear.' It would later be recorded in the
minutes of the meeting that Runge had not received any
money.[18] This behaviour of Kriegsgerichtsrat Jorns cannot
be explained by his sympathy for Pabst and his officers
alone. As Levi suspected in the first Jorns trial, in 1928–29,
Jorns must have been involved with the officers in some
way or another.[19]

---

in the paper, BA-SAPMO, *Nachlass Noske*, NL 56/3, 5. The letter allows us
to conclude that the wedding and party took place on 17 February. In Pabst's
'Ahnenpass', the Nazi-era certificate proving one's 'Aryan' background, the
date of marriage is listed as 27 February 1919, BA-SAPMO, *Nachlass Pabst*,
NY 4035/1, 3.

17 See Pabst's taped interview, in which he claims: 'I sent Runge away!'
The forged passports are in BA-MA, PH 8V/vol. 4, 56.

18 BA-MA, PH 8V/vol. 4, 57. See also Runge's infamous letter dated
6 January 1929, BA-MA, PH 8V/ vol. 8, 123–30; reprinted with slight mod-
ifications in *Die Freiheit* 13, 9 January 1921.

19 See *Das Tagebuch*, vol. 9, 1st half of 1928, 471–3, author: Berthold
Jacob Salomon (1898–1944). On Jacob's fate see Jost Nikolaus Willi, *Der
Fall Jacob-Wesemann*, Basel: PhD dissertation, 1972, 6–51; *Berliner Tageblatt*,
20 April 1929; Josef Bernstein, 'Mit Reichsanwalt Jorns vor Gericht', *Das
Tagebuch*, vol. 10, 1st half of 1929, 676; LAB, Rep. 58, no. 59, vol. 2, 110ff;
Leipziger Volkszeitung, 14 February 1930. See also *Dokumentation SDR*, 1168;
Berliner Tageblatt, 8, 9, 25 July 1930; *Vorwärts*, 8 July 1930; *Montag Morgen*, 14
July 1930; *Der Mord*, 169; BA-MA, PH 8V/vol. 24, verdict, 211; Dr Wenzel,
Dokumentation SDR, 1169, Stuttgart district court verdict,107, *Dokumentation
SDR*, 1051. Verdicts from the first three Jorns trials and further materials can
be found in LAB, Rep. 58, no. 59, 7 vols; see also BA-MA, PH 8V/vol. 24.

Secretly taken photograph from the second Jorns trial in February 1930. Wilhelm Pieck stands on the left, Josef Bornstein (1899–1952) sits in the far background.

Jorns had sought to launch a libel action against *Das Tagebuch* and its co-publisher Josef Bornstein for an anonymous article which accused him of, among other things, aiding and abetting the murderers. Paul Levi took up Bornstein's defence and was thus able to view the relevant police files, through which he managed to prove that Jorns had in fact assisted the perpetrators. The state prosecutor twice made the mistake of referring to the joint plaintiff and lawyer Jorns as 'the accused'. The court concurred with Levi's remarks, finding sufficient evidence to rule that Jorns had aided and abetted Rosa Luxemburg's murderers

Also informative are the newspaper clipping collections of the Reich Court from February to July 1930, *Gen. Akten* II 147 b, BA-Berlin and those of the *Stahlhelm*, BA-Berlin, 61 Sta 1, no. 2040. Photos from the court room in the second Jorns trial, *Blick in die Welt*, 8 February 1930, BA-SAPMO, NL 1/19, 117f. An excellent introduction is contained in *Der Mord*, 133–78.

while serving as the investigating magistrate. The trial and verdict both received a great deal of public attention.

Jorns promptly lodged an appeal. The libel action entered its second round before the third large criminal chamber of the first Berlin district court on 27 January 1930. Levi once again represented Bornstein, but before long fell ill and died, most likely by suicide. Bornstein now took responsibility for his own defence. The state prosecutor, who had not supported Jorns's appeal, filed for Bornstein's acquittal. Jorns reacted by insulting his colleagues. This would lead to a conflict between the joint plaintiff, Jorns, and the main plaintiff, the chief prosecutor, which culminated in the latter accusing Jorns of besmirching the honour of the judiciary for his own political reasons. The court once more ruled that proof of Jorns's complicity had been provided, and

A political cartoon printed in the *Montag Morgen*, 14 July 1930, mocking the second Jorns trial.

Jorns was disgraced a second time. Undaunted, he lodged yet another appeal, this time to the country's highest instance: the Reich Supreme Court in Leipzig. That illustrious body went to great lengths to determine that, according to legal principles, evidence of conscious aiding and abetting was insufficient to prove that an investigating official had aided and abetted! Furnished with this ruling,

Report in the 4 February 1930 issue of the *Welt am Abend*.

a fresh round of negotiations unfolded before a district court in Berlin. As was to be expected, the court accepted Jorns's claim that a 'slip of the minute-taker's pen' had turned '1/4 hour' into '24 hours'. The circumstance that Jorns had edited decrees issued by Captain von Pflugk-Harttung, who was involved in Liebknecht's murder, was also seen as innocuous, being of no 'relevance to the matter'. The result: although the fourth superior criminal court had proved unable to conceal the objective deficiency of Jorns's administration, the Reich Supreme Court concluded that Jorns's actions had been 'subjectively without fault'! Jorns was thus, legally speaking, exonerated.

Logically, the judge in Stuttgart's district court in the trial of Souchon vs. Süddeutscher Rundfunk, Hans Bausch

and Dieter Ertel in 1970 would refer back to this 'excul-
pation' in order to certify for Jorns 'that no indications of
falsification or distortion of recorded witness testimonies
or influencing of witnesses exist'.

Pabst, on the other hand, would confirm in 1966[20] that he
himself had practically been Jorns's judge and even participated in the questioning of witnesses. Jorns had been tasked
with preventing a trial by 'correcting' the witness testimonies, and did his best to achieve this. 'He accomplished his
difficult task splendidly.'

---

20 See document 1, p. 171.

8
The Trial

One of the most shameless, mendacious trials in German legal history began on 8 May 1919. Powerful units of the GKSD had cordoned off the criminal court in Moabit, while tickets to watch the proceedings were scalped on the black market at inflated prices.[1]

The defendants entered the court through the same door as the judges, into a room still presided by a gigantic portrait of Kaiser Wilhelm II. They got along  well throughout the course of the trial, even chatting with their relatives in the observation room during breaks.[2]

The trial was characterized above all by the fact that every one of the men in uniform told lies, so much so

---

1 Original entry ticket in BA-SAPMO, NY 4001/18 (previously NL 1/18), 2.

2 As confirmed by the chairman Ehrhardt, BA-MA, PH 8V/vol. 13, 180.

'that the balconies began to bend'.[3] One might say that the higher the rank, the bigger the lies. They were opposed by the heavily intimidated staff of the Hotel Eden, of whom several – including the chambermaid, Anna Belger, and both seventeen-year-old waiters, Mistelski and Krupp – worked up the courage to report what they had seen, and to stand by their claims.

The guarded entrance to the courtroom. The man wearing a hat could be the lawyer Fritz Grünspach.

Anna Belger had heard officers speaking of a 'greeting' for Liebknecht in the Tiergarten. The waiters identified the instigator of Runge's rifle-butt blows as Captain Petri, who had not even been summoned before the court as a witness, let alone a defendant. Following the testimony of former observer Wegmann, a wave of fear swept over the hotel staff. They had stated that they were 'afraid of the crowd below'. In this context, Wegmann reminded his audience of the Femenmorde, politically-motivated assassinations common in the early years of the Weimar Republic. The important notes taken by the observer had 'disappeared' during a search of the Executive Council

---

3   This phrase was uttered by Paul Levi, which Günther Nollau returned to in his witness testimony to the Stuttgart district court in 1970; Levi, *Jorns-Prozess*, 45; minutes of Nollau's testimony before the Stuttgart district court on 12 December 1969, *Dokumentation SDR*, 844.

premises ordered by Pabst, concurrent with his arrest of the Council's members in response to the railroad strikes on 27 June 1919.[4]

The trial's crowning moment, however, came when Wilhelm Canaris, a friend of Pabst and the accused Kaleu von Pflugk-Harttung, was appointed as presiding judge. Canaris commented on the case in an official capacity in 1931, indicating that he had been appointed because 'the parties involved had assured him of their trust'. By 'parties involved' he most certainly did not mean the victims' grieving friends and relatives. He explained the fact that he (as judge!) visited the accused in prison on grounds that he had to speak with Pflugk-Harttung about the Einwohnerwehren, or Citizens' Defence.[5]

Pabst would later admit that it was Canaris – in cahoots with him and Jorns – who pulled the strings in the trial, which itself had been a rather pathetic affair, somehow beneath his '*niveau*'.[6] Chairman Ehrhardt, 'an overly soft man',[7] was evidently not fully informed of the plan, but happily joined in the stonewalling in order to deflect any and all suspicion from his division. It was for this reason that the wildly unbelievable story told by the Pflugk-Harttung brothers and the naval squadron about the car trouble in the Tiergarten and the bid for escape of a badly injured

---

4   According to the *Berliner Tageblatt*, 20 April 1929; *Vorwärts*, 21 April 1929. Pabst, *Memoirs*, 126. Belger and the waiters' testimony in BA-MA, PH 8V/vol. 13, 229ff, 329ff, 345ff. See also Engel et al., *Groß-Berliner Arbeiter*, vol. 3, doc. 84.

5   BA-MA, PH 8V/vol. 4, 117; telephone note from Corvette Captain Fliess on 31 January 1931, BA-MA, RM 6/267, *Handakte Canaris*, 38.

6   See document I in the appendix to this volume.

7   Ibid.

Liebknecht (foolish enough to try to run away with a bleeding head wound), was accepted at face value, and those who fired the shots — von Pflugk-Harttung, Stiege, Schulze, and von Ritgen — declared not guilty.[8]

Had another young naval officer named Ernst von Weizsäcker respected the truth, he would have been obliged to inform the court what he confided to his diary on 16 January: 'Lieutenant Commander von Pflugk-Harttung was in the naval cabinet today and recounted, in return for the promise of absolute secrecy, that

Ernst von Weizsäcker (1882–1951). State Secretary at the Foreign Office and diplomat, sentenced to seven years in prison at the Nuremberg Trials in 1948. Pardoned in 1950.

during Liebknecht's transfer to prison he had faked car trouble in the Tiergarten and then took Liebknecht by the arm to lead him; intentionally let him go, in order to give him a chance to try to escape, and then after briefly turning away shot him in the back; Liebknecht was hit and killed by multiple shots. I advised Pflugk to flee.'[9]

Liebknecht's murder, at least as far as this testimony is concerned, would have been solved. In Luxemburg's case,

---

8   In order to save face, Jorns called for the death penalty for the gunmen on charges of illegal use of a weapon. Pabst, who had let Jorns in on the plan, gave him a free hand in the matter. See document I in the appendix to this volume; Pabst's letter to Ertel dated 28 October 1968, *Dokumentation SDR*, 184; see also the slightly different handwritten draft in BA-MA, N 620/21.

9   Ernst von Weizsäcker's diary entry in Hill, *Weizsäcker-Papiere*, 325.

on the other hand, the testimony of the uniformed witnesses would lead to great confusion.[10]

The escorting men Weber and Grantke testified that Vogel had stood on the footboard and shot Rosa Luxemburg. Infantryman Poppe, who had ridden along on the footboard, hesitated to make a definitive statement, but believed he had seen Vogel inside the vehicle. The driver Janschkow and his passenger Hall, on the other hand, who Vogel knew from the Bürgerwehr, stated that Vogel had been standing on the backrest of the front seat, supporting himself on the two of them and speaking with them, when the shot was fired. Something even more peculiar came next: both the escorts as well as Vogel spoke of an unidentified person, allegedly a naval officer in uniform, who was also present but whom Jorns had been unable to locate, although Janschkow ran into him in the Hotel Eden the day after the murder and claimed to have encountered him a second time on the tram. Vogel refused to testify concerning his identity.[11] Despite Jorns's intensive contact with Pabst, the naval officer could not be found. Nevertheless, Jorns assumed that Vogel had fired the shot.

Yet because Luxemburg's corpse had still not been located at this time,[12] and the precise cause of her death (Runge's blows with his rifle, or the gunshot) could not be

---

10   BA-MA, PH 8V/vol. 14, 571–98, vol. 15, 609–703, 730–59.

11   BA-MA, PH 8V/vol. 15, 743f, Janschkow's testimony; 657, Vogel's testimony.

12   The brave diver Alfred Kock, whom Jorns only sent to search the Landwehr Canal following a tip from Hugo Haase, fished three corpses (two female and one male) and seventy rifles from the roughly 400 metres of murky water between the S-train and the Lichtenstein bridges, but did not find Rosa Luxemburg's remains. BA-MA, PH 8V/vol. 3, 185f, vol. 15, 783.

A reconstruction of the proceedings for television in 1969. Hubert Suschka portrays the lawyer for the defence, Grünspach, Gerd Baltus (on the left, with moustache) portrays First Lieutenant Vogel, and Karl Walter Diess (second from the right) portrays Horst von Pflugk-Harttung. On the far right is Friedrich G. Beckhaus, in the role of Runge the hussar.

ascertained, Jorns's closing speech was able to toe a classic legal thin line: 'We are thus presented with the curious circumstance that the death of Frau Rosa Luxemburg was without a doubt caused by the actions of one of the two accused, but we cannot say which of the two committed the deed. Thus, in Runge's case, only the attempt would be present, and we can only convict First Lieutenant Vogel for attempting a punishable deed, namely a factually impossible attempt, as the *terminus technicum* [*sic*] for this is known.'[13]

There was thus a dead body still floating around somewhere in the Landwehr Canal, but there were no murderers,

---

13   Here, Jorns 'strictly' followed the Reich Court's assessment that the individual who fired on a corpse was to be prosecuted for attempted murder. BA-MA, PH 8V/vol. 17, 955.

just two men who had committed attempted murder. The court of comrades-in-arms was even 'more radical' in this instance. It acquitted Vogel of attempted murder, on the assumption that the unknown naval officer, the 'seventh man' in or around the automobile, had fired the shots.[14] By assuming this, the court could deliver mild verdicts in the Luxemburg case: for, among other things, attempted murder, Runge received two years in prison. Vogel was declared not guilty of attempted murder and sentenced to two years and four months in prison for, among other things, disposing of a corpse.[15]

---

14 BA-MA, PH 8V/vol. 17, 1036ff.

15 Ibid., 1035.

9
Vogel's Escape and 'Pursuit'

On 19 May 1919, a few days after the end of the trial, the Berlin newspaper *BZ am Mittag* reported that First Lieutenant Vogel had 'escaped from custody with the assistance of an officer yet to be identified'. The following day it transpired that one Lieutenant Lindemann had appeared in the Moabit prison on 17 May and presented a certificate bearing the 'carefully forged' signature of Kriegsgerichtsrat Jorns and an official GKSD stamp. Ulrich von Ritgen admits in his unpublished memoirs to falsifying the signature.[1]

Vogel was promptly released.[2] Both officers stepped into an automobile which roared away and disappeared. Given that 'the strictest automobile checks' were being carried

---

1 BA-MA, PH 8V/vol. 19, 3, von Ritgen in a taped interview from the 1960s. I thank his widow, Frau Elisabeth von Ritgen, for permitting me to view these materials.

2 See report filed by Rühle von Lilienstern on 18 May 1919, BA-MA, PH 8V/vol. 19, 1f; Pabst's largely falsified report from 21 May 1919, 38; as well as the testimony given by Oskar Heidemann, the representative of the Moabit prison commandant von Zitzewitz, 18–20. See also *Berliner Volkszeitung*, 19 May 1919.

```
Gericht d.G.K.K.                          Berlin den 15. kai 1919.
III.J.Nr: 321.


        An den Kommandanten des

                Zellengefängnisses M o a b i t .

                Der Untersuchungsgefangene Oberleutnant
Vogel ist zwecks Überführung in das Strafgefängniss Tegel
dem Überbringer auszuliefern.
```

The pass with Jorns's convincingly forged signature.

out 'throughout Greater Berlin', it was hard to fathom how the vehicle could have slipped through.[3] The mystery was compounded when it also emerged that parliamentary deputy Oskar Cohn had contacted the Ministry of War and the Reich Chancellery on 14 May, to alert them that fake passports had been produced for the purpose of First Lieutenant Vogel's escape.[4]

Noske summoned Pabst and informed him of Cohn's warnings. Pabst exhibited grave concern and 'while still

---

3   *Berliner Volkszeitung*, 20 May 1919.

4   Dr Oskar Cohn (1869–1934), lawyer, USPD. Cohn had learned from an acquaintance that two passports for Holland had 'been arranged'. That same day, Noske issued a dramatically worded order to the 1st Group Command of the German Army, von Lüttwitz's division, which commanded the GKSD, in which he insisted 'that no freedom be permitted for the accused'. BA-MA, PH 8V/vol. 19, 119f. Cohn's statement to the public prosecutor, *Berliner Volkszeitung*, 21 May 1919, see also Pabst's report dated 21 May 1919, BA-MA, PH 8V/vol. 19, 57.

in the minister's anteroom, gave orders first by telephone and later again in writing' that Vogel be transferred to the northern military prison. But – surprise, surprise! – that institution was both over capacity and infested with lice, to which they did not wish to expose the prisoner. Thus, they had to wait until delousing was complete.[5] Unfortunately, Vogel escaped in the meantime.

Conspicuously anxious to recapture their infamous fugitive, the GKSD offered a public reward of 3,000 marks.[6] Yet the investigation conducted by this extremely independent judiciary proved as unsuccessful as usual. Replacing the lead investigator – Jorns had moved on to other duties and was succeeded by a court-martial officer named Spatz (probably an alias for Hans Günther von Dincklage, later a Nazi spy in France) – was of little help. For Spatz, also in the GKSD, was not in a position to uncover Vogel's whereabouts or the particulars of his escape. Like Jorns, the man was a pearl of the military justice system, a master of hot air – he interrogated witnesses by the dozen, typed up and stamped stacks of paper, and ultimately compiled four thick volumes.[7]

One thing Spatz, alias von Dincklage, was generous with when it mattered was his time. He was in no hurry to issue an arrest warrant for Vogel (waiting nine days after

---

5   Pabst's order, BA-MA, PH 8V/vol. 4, 234; see also Heidemann's statement, BA-MA, PH 8V/ vol. 19, 19; as well as the judgement in the third Jorns trial, LAB, Rep. 58, no. 59, vol. 4, 316.

6   The original poster, signed by the 'Court of the GardeKav. (Schützen-) Korps' claims, several days after Vogel was acquitted of attempted murder, that he had been in preventive custody 'for the murder of Frau Rosa Luxemburg', BA-MA, PH 8V/vol. 4, 217; see also *Berliner Volkszeitung*, 19 May 1919.

7   BA-MA, PH 8V/vols 19–22.

the escape), which he dispatched to the German mission in Copenhagen.[8] He had to be helped along by the press to find out where Vogel was currently hiding. An article appeared in *Die Freiheit* on 28 May, reporting that: 1. Vogel was in Holland. 2. He had been given a passport under the name 'Kurt Velsen' from the Ministry of War's passport office. 3. The motor car that so effortlessly whisked the two officers through Berlin belonged to Hermann Janschkow, who also drove the car in which Rosa Luxemburg was murdered. The GKSD had purchased a vehicle from him after the murder, leading *Die Freiheit* to speculate they may have been one and the same automobile. The two men primarily responsible were Pabst and Grabowsky.[9]

Now things were too much even for the *Vorwärts*, which denounced a scandal without precedent. 'A government that tolerates such a mockery of the administration of the law by a handful of insubordinate officers will be forced to forfeit any and all authority in the country', it thundered, demanding that 'it now wring the neck of this clique with an iron fist'.[10] But the Scheidemann government was either unable or unwilling to wriggle out of the military justice system's web. Although Scheidemann insisted that 'all facts reported by *Die Freiheit* must be carefully inspected as quickly as possible',[11] he never thought to deploy the state

8   BA-Berlin, Auswärtiges Amt, *Akten betreffend die strafrechtliche Verfolgung des Oberleutnants Vogel* (henceforth 'AA-Vogel'), no. 27402/1, 2, arrested warrant dated 26 May 1919.

9   *Die Freiheit*, 28 May 1919.

10   *Vorwärts*, 29 May 1919.

11   BA-Berlin, AA-Vogel, no. 27402/1, 18, excerpt from the minutes of the Reich government meeting on 31 May 1919.

prosecutor for this task. On the contrary: with seemingly infinite trust, the authorities allowed themselves to be led down the garden path by the friends of the GKSD. It was a never-ending story: when the GKSD finally inquired as to Vogel's whereabouts at the German legation in Holland,[12] the envoy Friedrich Rosen, who was genuinely ignorant of the affair, responded that 'nothing is known of Vogel's presence in Holland'. [13] This settled the matter as far as the GKSD was concerned. However, *Die Freiheit* on 31 May and the *Berliner Lokalanzeiger* on 5 June brought new information to light, which rekindled the tension. It seemed that a man had appeared at the Foreign Ministry on 13 May 1919, presenting a passport pass under the name Kurt Velsen issued by the presidium of the police (dated 3 May). The man identified himself as an appointee of the German Armistice Commission (Deutsche Waffenstillstandskommission, or WaKo) headed by Matthias Erzberger, and explained that Herr Kurt Velsen also worked for the commission and needed to travel to Holland on WaKo business.

A passport from the Armistice Commission with the signature 'Erzberger' had indeed been presented, which meant that Erzberger had some explaining to do. In a session of the Reich Chancellery, Erzberger made 'confidential disclosures concerning the person who, according to his information, had participated in the falsification of the passport'. Who this person was is not recorded in the minutes of the session. Liepmann, who also received a forged passport under the name 'Lohmann', stated in the

---

12   Ibid., no. 27402/1, telegram dated 28 May 1919.
13   BA-Berlin, AA-Vogel, no. 27402/1, 13, telegram dated 29 May 1919.

second Jorns trial that Erzberger had known about the use of the WaKo passport. Canaris even claimed in 1931 that Erzberger intentionally provided the document to facilitate Vogel's escape. Pabst would offer a similar account in his own memoirs.[14]

The Dutch General Consulate allegedly issued the necessary visa around the same time. It soon became clear that this news was in fact true, although the presidium of the police had never issued such a pass, the prerequisite to acquire a passport for traveling abroad. The 'police presidium pass' (issued on 3 May) presented by the mystery person must have been an excellent forgery, since no government office managed to spot it.[15] Citing a report from the Dutch newspaper *De Telegraaf*, Rosen would write from the Foreign Ministry on 1 June: 'In this case, the Ministry is not at fault. For the passport to obtain a visa was presented by a person who must have appeared utterly reliable.' Where this 'utterly reliable person' came from had been announced in the *Algemeen Handelsblad* as early as 31 May. There was only one office that, due to the war and the requirements of espionage, possessed 'the necessary technical means' to falsify documents to perfection: the

---

14   BA-Berlin, AA-Vogel, no. 27402/1, 65, Consulate Secretary Ernst's testimony, as well as 66. R 43 I 2676, 55, minutes of the Reich government meeting on 29 May 1919; *Vorwärts* 47, 6 February 1930; *Welt am Abend*, 4 February 1930; BA-MA, RM 6/267, *Handakte Canaris*, 50. Nearly identical: Grabowsky, ibid., 22; Pabst, *Memoirs*, 81f. Matthias Erzberger (1875–1921) was murdered by Heinrich Schulz and Heinrich Tillessen, two members of the proto-fascist Geheimorganisation Consul (OC) led by Corvette Captain Hermann Ehrhardt.

15   This is confirmed by messages from the desk clerk at the office of Public Prosecutor Weismann; BA-Berlin, AA-Vogel, no. 27402/1, 65–7 and 70–3.

General Staff in Berlin. Shortly thereafter, former People's Deputy Hugo Haase would tell the chief press officer of the Reich Chancellery, Rauscher,[16] the name of the man who he was convinced had 'assisted the escape': Wilhelm Canaris, the judge in the Luxemburg/Liebknecht trial, a member of the GKSD general staff and an adjutant of Noske. On Scheidemann's insistence, Canaris was then arrested by General von Lüttwitz on 10 May (bypassing Noske, who was conveniently not in Berlin at the time), and released three days later – citing lack of evidence, combined with a blatant threat to overthrow Scheidemann.[17] Canaris was likewise spared the lice in the Moabit prison which had contributed to Vogel's escape. He was pleasantly housed in the Berlin City Palace with the Loewenfeld naval brigade, of which he was of course also a member.

Despite the government's assurances, the GKSD court and comrade-in-arms Spatz were entrusted with further inquiries into the Canaris 'passport affair'.[18] Spatz organized another legal circus, busily questioning Scheidemann and holding police line-ups.[19] Needless to say, the investigation came to nothing. Spatz, who like Jorns was in cahoots with the murderers, finally produced a dodgy alibi for the suspect: Canaris had been in Pforzheim, getting engaged to Erika Wang, on the day of Vogel's escape. The investigation

---

16   BA-MA, PH 8V/vol. 21, 36f, Rauscher's testimony. See also Haase's letter to the GKSD, 21 July 1919, BA-MA, PH 8V/vol. 20, 125.

17   Letter from von Lüttwitz to Scheidemann dated 13 June 1919, BA-Koblenz R 43 I 2676, 63f; BA-MA, RM 6/267, *Handakte Canaris*, 38.

18   Minutes of the Reich government meeting dated 29 May 1919, BA-Koblenz, R 43 I 2676, 55.

19   BA-MA, PH 8V/vol. 19, 167f.

was, predictably, closed.[20] Spatz naturally never thought to organize a line-up with Canaris for the guards from the Moabit prison who had seen 'Lindemann', and no one held it against him.

A major scandal broke out seven years later during an inquiry convened to investigate 'the causes of the German collapse in the year 1918', on 23 January 1926.[21] Canaris had been called to testify by the Reich minister of defence, Otto Geßler. When it emerged that he was the same Canaris 'who served as an observer in the trial of Liebknecht and Luxemburg's murderers, and the man accused of having contributed the most to Vogel's escape at the time', pandemonium broke out. Canaris responded: 'I have nothing to say regarding the personal matters being alleged. I am a representative of the naval leadership here, and will not tread upon this personal terrain' – by which he meant his participation in the murder plot.

Parliamentary deputy Arthur Rosenberg took a while to make himself heard: 'As I said, it is an unprecedented event that Herr Reich Minister of Defence Dr Geßler thinks it's a good idea to dispatch a representative to this board in such a difficult historical and legal matter against whom the gravest accusations of a criminal nature have been raised. The explanation given by Corvette Captain

---

20   On 23 December 1919; BA-MA, PH 8V/vol. 21, 187ff.

21   The following quotes are taken from Albrecht Phillip (ed.), *Das Werk des Untersuchungsausschusses der verfassunggebenden Deutschen Nationalversammlung und des deutschen Reichstages 1919–1926. 4. Reihe: Die Ursachen des deutschen Zusammenbruchs im Jahre 1918*, Berlin: Deutsche Verlagsgesellschaft für Politik und Geschichte, 1928 (henceforth '*WUA*'), vol. 9, I,139ff.

Canaris amounts, for every objectively minded person, to a confirmation of the accusation.' Canaris left the hall shortly after, stating that the thoroughly unjustified attacks against him could be easily cleared up by sending an enquiry to his superior authority. Herr Geßler, from the 'superior authority', responded days later with one of his grandiose denials: the charge that Canaris 'had participated in the escape of First Lieutenant Vogel is utterly unfounded, as has been confirmed by a court trial initiated by my official predecessor.'[22] And thus, the affair came full circle: the court trial initiated by Noske was of course the same as that so officiously conducted by comrade-in-arms Kriegsgerichtsrat Spatz, yet curiously without his probes reaching any kind of result.

The hollowness of Reich Minister of Defence Geßler's denials would be revealed in 1931, during the third Jorns trial, when the chairman of the National Federation of German Officers, a lawyer known as Dr Bredereck, testified that 30,000 marks had been made available for the Pflugk-Harttung brothers' escape. Canaris had been present when the money was given to their sister.[23] This allegation led to a further denial from Reich Minister of Defence Groener, in a text largely composed by Pabst's propaganda chief Grabowsky.[24]

22   *WUA*, vol. 9, I, 165. Arthur Rosenberg (1889–1943) was a historian, a member of the Communist Party for some time, and the author of a standard reference work on the Weimar Republic.

23   Bredericek's testimony in the third Jorns trial, as reported in the *Vorwärts*, 23 January 1931. See also Canaris's indications, BA-MA, RM 6/267, *Handakte Canaris*, 22.

24   BA-MA, RM 6/267, *Handakte Canaris*, 22f and 48f. Wilhelm Groener (1867–1939) rendered outstanding services on the railways in the First World

Forty-seven years later, Waldemar Pabst would finally confirm what had been suspected for decades: Canaris was not only the man responsible for organizing Vogel's forged passport, he was also the ominous Lieutenant Lindemann who had taken Vogel out of prison.[25]

The director of Munich's Institute of Contemporary History from 1959 to 1972, Helmut Krausnick, who in the 1930s lived in the same building as Vogel (Waltraudstraße 36, in Berlin's Zehlendorf neighbourhood) and conversed with him, would confirm in the 1960s that Vogel's assistant in the escape had been Canaris.

Pabst indicated that the commandant of the Moabit prison, von Zitzewitz, had called him: Vogel desired to give new testimony, namely, that he had been operating under orders. Now the danger emerged that Vogel, terrified of being snatched from prison by the Spartacists, would tell the truth.[26] He therefore had to disappear. Pabst and Canaris together planned how it could be done.[27] This conspiracy led to what was surely an unprecedented event in German legal history: a judge helping a defendant to escape, going so far as to obtain the necessary papers for him.

War and campaigned for cooperation with the trade unions during the conflict. He became head of the Supreme Army Command in November 1918. Around the turn of 1918–19, he acted as one of Ebert's allies in the military against the revolution. Pabst did not like him, wrongly judging him to be too 'weak'. Groener began developing a new German world power policy early on, and served as Reich Minister of Defence from 1928 to 1932.

25   See document I in the appendix to this volume. Heinz Höhne's personal disclosure. See also Höhne, *Canaris*, 608, n. 123.

26   See document I in the appendix to this volume. See also Liepmann's testimony in the third Jorns trial, BA-MA, PH 8V/ vol. 24 or LAB, Rep. 58, no. 59, vol. 4. Also reprinted in *Der Mord*, 177.

27   Pabst, recorded interview.

Yet the imprisoned officers were taken care of. For their own 'protection', they were given hand grenades, machine guns and flamethrowers as a precautionary measure. The Moabit prison and its commandant von Zitzewitz were subordinate to the Reinhard Regiment, which in turn was part of the GKSD. Wilhelm Reinhard (1869–1955) would later become an SS Obergruppenführer.

But let us return to the hunt for Vogel. Rosen, honestly preoccupied with solving the case, ordered searches across Holland, to be reported back to the Foreign Office almost daily. It became known that Vogel was in fact in Holland on 6 June, hiding out in the German foreign section in The Hague.[28] While court martial officer Spatz struggled to make progress,[29] Scheidemann cabled Rosen to tell him he should compel Vogel to return to Berlin, accompanied by a public official. Should he refuse, further measures to ensure his extradition would be undertaken.[30] Rosen was able to report on 8 June that Vogel was in an internment camp, where Dutch authorities had placed him after he re-emerged.

Rosen reckoned that because Vogel had already been deprived of his freedom, 'the order given to me to exhort him to return to Germany voluntarily can be considered dealt with.'[31] The entire affair could be laid to rest. Five weeks later, on 21 June 1919, freshly-minted Chancellor

---

28   BA-Berlin, AA-Vogel, no. 27402/1, 33.

29   BA-Berlin, AA-Vogel, no. 27402/1, 38 and 43.

30   BA-Berlin, AA-Vogel, no. 27402/1, 46a, telegram from the Foreign Office to Rosen dated 3 June 1919.

31   BA-Berlin, AA-Vogel, no. 27402/1, 58, letter from Rosen to the Foreign Office dated 13 June 1919.

The Berlin City Palace in December 1918 flying the red flag, and in June 1919 flying the Imperial War Flag.

of the Reich Gustav Bauer inquired of the Foreign Office whether they could update him on 'the state of efforts towards [Vogel's] extradition'. The answer came: 'The GKSD court is looking into the prospect of sending the papers necessary to justify the extradition petition to the Dutch government'.[32] Once again, nothing happened, except that Rosen received a letter from one Herr Husborg in Copenhagen, asking for guidance: 'Funds have been sent to me from various Danish and Swedish families to be delivered to First Lieutenant Herr Kurt Vogel who is interned in Holland. I most respectfully ask the German Legation whether Herr First Lieutenant Vogel can be given the money from here.'[33] Two weeks later, on 16 July, Rosen told the Foreign Office that an order concerning the extradition

32   BA-Berlin, AA-Vogel, no. 27402/1, 69, letter from the Foreign Office to the Reich Chancellery dated 27 June 1919.

33   BA-Berlin, AA-Vogel, no. 27402/1, 78, letter from Husborg to Rosen dated 3 July 1919.

was yet to be presented. Shortly after, the Chancellor of the Reich again sought an update on the state of the extradition request.[34] The Foreign Office answered ten days later that Vogel's extradition could not proceed, because the GKSD court was withholding the necessary documents.[35] After an entire month had passed, Spatz decided to present a draft for the arrest warrant. By then, it was 21 August 1919.[36]

Yet the draft proved ineffectual, the Foreign Office claimed, as it referred to a 'misdemeanour' committed while in the service of the military, something not covered by the extradition treaty with Holland. A new arrest warrant was ordered, which was to refer to crimes of a non-military nature.[37] Spatz could be sure that such objections would be raised thanks to his cleverly formulated draft. He continued to stall so doggedly that an honest colleague from the military court remonstrated with him: 'Spatz explained to me in his own long-winded fashion what difficulties he had had in taking care of the matter… In response, I observed that in my opinion he would have reached his goal faster and more easily had he not sought to circumvent the authorities so much, and instead taken a look at the conditions for [Vogel's] extradition issued by the Ministry of War.'[38]

---

34   BA-Berlin, AA-Vogel, no. 27402/1, 82, letter from the Reich Chancellery to the Foreign Office dated 19 July 1919.

35   BA-Koblenz, R 43 I 2676, 81, letter from the Foreign Office to the Reich Chancellery dated 29 July 1919.

36   BA-Koblenz, R 43 I 2676, 122ff, BA-Berlin, AA-Vogel, no. 27402/1, 90ff.

37   BA-Koblenz, R 43 I 2676, 97f, letter to the GKSD dated 8 September 1919.

38   BA-MA, PH 8V/vol. 22, 54ff.

The colleague also expressed outrage that Spatz had gone on vacation without dealing with the issue, and afterwards had simply abandoned it.

The stalling tactics worked. The Reich Chancellery sent another message on 22 September, politely requesting 'a prompt answer concerning the state of the affair'.[39]

On 27 September the WTB wire service put it out that Vogel was in Montevideo, but envoy Rosen reassured his superiors that the fugitive was still in Holland.[40] The infinitely patient Reich Chancellery made another enquiry concerning 'the state of the extradition request' on 16 October. Again, nothing happened.[41]

The Reich Ministry of Defence would 'intervene' on 10 November. Noske, sitting in Canaris's anteroom, ordered his chief of staff, von Gilsa, to claim the following in a letter: Spatz was in ongoing contact with the Foreign Office and had been informed that chances of an extradition were slim.[42] This was an outright lie.

The Foreign Office retorted angrily on 21 November, objecting that the Ministry of Defence's letter had not accurately conveyed the status of the Vogel extradition, since Spatz had not dispatched a draft of the arrest warrant until 21 August. The Foreign Office's concerns were not addressed, nor does any further written correspondence

---

39   BA-Berlin, AA-Vogel, no. 27402/1, 99.

40   BA-Berlin, AA-Vogel, no. 27402/1, 104, telegram from Rosen to the Foreign Office dated 8 October 1919.

41   BA-MA, PH 8V/vol. 22, 53–55.

42   BA-Berlin, AA-Vogel, no. 27402/1, 108, letter from von Gilsa to the Reich Chancellery dated 10 November 1919.

transpire.[43] Ultimately, the court of Reichswehr Brigade 15 that was now responsible (the GKSD had been dissolved, but Spatz still served as director of the investigation) ran out of options: it was forced to issue an arrest warrant for Vogel. Curtly and succinctly, and contrary to the judgement issued by the field court martial, this warrant accused Vogel of the murder of Rosa Luxemburg. However, Spatz added, Vogel could not be extradited if the sentence from 14 May 1919 was ratified, as that only referred to dereliction of duty and disposing of a corpse.[44]

43   BA-Berlin, AA-Vogel, no. 27402/1, 109f, letter from the Foreign Office to the Reich Ministry of Defence and Reich Chancellery dated 21 November 1919.

44   BA-Berlin, AA-Vogel, no. 27402/1, 113f, letter from Spatz to the Foreign Office.

10

Passing the Buck

This objection hinted at something else, which had occurred in parallel to the above-mentioned events. After a surge of public outrage in response to the shameful verdict delivered by the military, the SPD Greater Berlin branch passed a unanimous motion demanding that the sentences not be ratified. The SPD members of the Berlin Executive Council demanded the same.[1] The government was clueless as to who would now confirm or overturn this grandiose sentence (although the SPD leadership never seriously considered the latter option). The initial consensus was that Friedrich Ebert, as President of the Reich and legal successor to the Kaiser, was responsible. He himself demurred, however, and 'tended towards the view' that the Prussian Ministry of State was responsible. The Ministry similarly declined, and thus the buck was passed to Gustav Noske, to whom Ebert had made minister of defence.[2]

---

1 According to *Die Freiheit* 236, 17 May 1919 and *Berliner Tageblatt*, 18 May 1919.

2 BA-Berlin, Reichs-Justizamt, *Akten betreffend die militärgerichtliche*

As had been the case in January 1919, Noske did not duck 'responsibility'. Although he stated in March that he would not involve himself in 'legal tinkering' and that articles of the law did not apply to him,[3] he could not afford to dispense with legal advice entirely. The Military Court of the Reich and the Reich Minister

The location where Rosa Luxemburg's corpse was found, as it appears today. The sluice between the Freiarchen and S-train bridges.

of Justice Schiffer were thus instructed to draft assessments which could help him make up his mind.[4] The assessors, however, confronted a changed circumstance: on the morning of Saturday 31 May 1919, a sluice-gate attendant had discovered a female corpse between the Freiarchen and S-Bahn bridges.[5] It was the body of Rosa Luxemburg.

One witness, a Social Democrat, recognized her and placed a phone call to the *Vorwärts*. Yet no report would appear in the paper on either Saturday or Sunday.[6] On Monday morning a brief note appeared which, as so often,

Untersuchung des Herganges bei der Tötung des Karl Liebknecht und der Rosa Luxemburg, Strafverfahren gegen Runge und Genossen (henceforth 'RJA-Tötung'), no. 3720, 61, letter from the Office of the President of the Reich dated 18 September 1919 as well as 12f, letter from the Reich Ministry of Justice dated 26 September 1919.

3   Noske in the National Assembly, 13 and 27 March 1919.

4   BA-MA, PH 8V/vol. 8, legal assessment of the High Reich Attorney at the Reich Military Court dated 12 July 1919, 2634. BA-Koblenz, R 43 I 2676, 105–114, legal assessment of the Reich Minister of Justice Schiffer dated 13 October 1919.

5   BA-MA, PH 8V/vol. 6, 9ff, esp. 15. Covering letter no. 116 of the Tiergarten Police Station on 31 May 1919 concerning the delivery of a corpse.

6   BA-SAPMO, NL 1/19, 99f, report by Otto Fritsch dated 28 February 1952.

only contained half-truths: a military patrol (*sic*) had discovered the corpse on 1 June (*sic*). The reason for this distortion was yet another suspicious, shady event: while relaxing in the house of the former head of the High Seas Fleet, Admiral von Holtzendorff, workers' movement leader Noske had been informed by excited party colleagues and like-minded comrades, Wolfgang Heine and Eugen Ernst, that 'she' had been found.[7] Noske immediately declared a gagging order (which he neglected to report) and had the remains shipped to his military friends in the Zossen detention centre, south of Berlin.

Even the corpse of Rosa Luxemburg was enough to inspire fear. Social Democrat Noske again finds bold words: 'I did not hold consultations concerning the legal permissibility of such a move.'[8] However, his initiative wounded the honour of Kriegsgerichtsrat Ehrhardt.

This 'insulted judiciary' (Noske's words) reproved the supreme command for interfering in his jurisdiction.[9] Corpse thief Noske, who normally took great pains to avoid raining on the GKSD's parade, scolded Ehrhardt right back.[10]

---

7   Gustav Noske, *Erlebtes aus Aufstieg und Niedergang einer Demokratie*, Offenbach-Main: Bollwerk-Verlag K. Drott, 1947, 86. As it happens, Pabst repeatedly made positive statements about the party right-winger Heine in his memoirs. Eugen Ernst (1864–1954), president of police by profession and Eichhorn's successor, catalyst for the January Uprising, was 'as caustic with his men as Blücher was' (Kessler, *Berlin in Lights*, 63), and made his services available to the Kapp putschists in March 1920. In 1946 he backed the forced merger of the KPD and the SPD into the Socialist Unity Party (SED) in the Soviet-occupied zone.

8   Noske, *Erlebtes*, 86.

9   BA-MA, PH 8V/vol. 6, 910, written complaint by Ehrhardt dated 2 June 1919.

10   Noske, *Erlebtes*, 86; Ehrhardt's testimony as reported in the *Vorwärts*, 7 February 1930.

Luxemburg's long-time friend and trusted secretary, Mathilde Jacob,[11] who suspected that Noske must 'have an interest in the lifeless body',[12] was now permitted by the snubbed Ehrhardt 'to take a doctor, chosen by us, to Zossen in my car, to assess the results of the forensic physician's autopsy'.[13] Yet her first choice – Theodor Liebknecht's representative, Dr Siegfried Weinberg – refused, arguing that to go along would be tantamount to acknowledging the legitimacy of the GKSD court.[14]

An excerpt from the autopsy findings of Privy Medical Councillor Dr Strassmann and the court doctor, Dr Fraenkel.

Jacob did not agree, as she understandably hoped to gain more information about 'the type of murder'. She desperately looked for support elsewhere: two doctors 'feared for

---

11   BA-MA, PH 8V/vol. 6, 30. Mathilde Jacob, like Maxim Zetkin, was subjected to Spatz's investigation; see BA-MA, PH 8V/vol. 7, 115f.

12   Mathilde Jacob, 'Von Rosa Luxemburg und ihren Freunden in Krieg und Revolution 1914–1919', edited by Sibylle Quack and Rüdiger Zimmermann, *Internationale wissenschaftliche Korrespondenz*, 24 (4), 1988, 503.

13   Jacob, 'Krieg und Revolution', 504.

14   See BA-MA, PH 8V/vol. 6, 10f, Weinberg's rejection letter to the GKSD dated 2 June 1919.

their lives', another changed his mind.[15] The autopsy thus took place without an independent medical examiner sent by Mathilde Jacob.

Privy Medical Examiner Dr Strassmann and his deputy Professor Dr Fraenckel began their investigation of the badly decomposed corpse on 3 June 1919. The conclusion was that Rosa Luxemburg had not been killed by the two blows from the butt of Runge's rifle, but rather by a gunshot fired at point-blank range.[16]

In that case, only Vogel or the mysterious unidentified naval officer could have been the culprit. The legal assessors could not overlook this fact in their 'appellate decision'. As was to be expected, both argued to confirm the verdicts against Runge and the crew of the Liebknecht transport (von Pflugk-Harttung and the rest), yet in Vogel's case they both urged a new hearing.[17]

The assessment issued by Minister of Justice Schiffer[18]

---

15   Jacob, 'Krieg und Revolution', 504.

16   BA-MA, PH 8V/vol. 7, 3641, autopsy findings of Privy Medical Examiner Dr Strassmann and deputy Dr Fraenckel, dated 3 June 1919, as well as vol. 6, 3749, secondary evaluation by Strassmann/Fraenckel dated 13/17 June 1919. See BA-SAPMO, NL 1/19, 69ff. Mathilde Jacob identified the corpse through a golden pendant and some scraps of blue velvet. In the minutes she also states: 'I would prefer not to view the photographs of the corpse.' (We have chosen not to reproduce the gruesome pictures here.) Fritz Strassmann (1858–1940) conducted autopsies on Karl Liebknecht as well as Foreign Minister Walther Rathenau, murdered in 1922, and later would give academic lectures on the topic of 'executions while escaping'. He later attempted to escape persecution as a Jew by being baptized.

17   BA-MA, PH 8V/vol. 8, legal assessment of senior Reich prosecutor at the Reich military court dated 12 July 1919, 33; BA-Koblenz, R 43 I 2676, 113f, legal assessment of Reich Minister of Justice Schiffer dated 13 October 1919.

18   Eugen Schiffer (1860–1954), member of the German Democratic Party (DDP), Finance Minister in 1919, Justice Minister 1919–21. Pabst

went further, diverging from the Reich Military Lawyer to state that Vogel had most likely fired the shot at Rosa Luxemburg, 'but cast-iron proof of guilt has not been provided'. It mentioned that this would be important 'should Vogel retrospectively give statements concerning the identity of the still unidentified officer who could potentially be the perpetrator alongside him'.[19] The Cabinet would follow the assessment on 7 October and ratify the verdicts against Runge, von Pflugk-Harttung and the rest. No firm decision about Vogel's fate was taken.[20] On 26 October 1919, Noske explicitly reserved the right to hold back his decision on this ratification until after Vogel's interrogation.[21]

Of course, thanks to Spatz, Vogel was still in Holland. On 4 December 1919, the anxious Rosen could finally announce that he had petitioned the Dutch government to extradite Vogel in line with his orders.[22] The WTB spread a rumour on 11 December that Vogel's sentence had been confirmed after all.

This sparked further confusion. The Reich Chancellery enquired on 24 January 1920 as to what decision the Dutch

---

also frequented Schiffer's home and was connected to the vice-chancellor's daughter. Personal testimony of Prof. Dr Johannes Erger.

19   BA-Koblenz, R 43 I 2676, 114, Schiffer's legal evaluation. The draft of the evaluation goes into more detail: 'It is especially taken into account whether perhaps new moments have emerged which seem fitting to disregard existing concerns against some witness testimonies [the accompanying soldiers from Luxemburg's transport].' BA-Berlin, RJA-Tötung, no. 3720, 72.

20   Ibid., 74, minutes of the Reich government meeting dated 7 October 1919.

21   Letter from Noske to the President of the Reich military court dated 26 October 1919, BA-Koblenz, R 43 I 2676, 119; also contained in BA-MA PH 8V/vol. 8, 34.

22   BA-Berlin, AA-Vogel, no. 27402/1, 121, letter from Rosen to Foreign Office dated 4 December 1919.

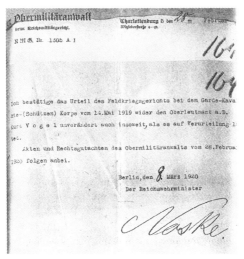

Noske's approval of the verdict.

had reached.[23] But the Dutch government appeared not to react. Vogel, meanwhile, did. He dispatched a cheeky legal memo, stating that he accepted the sentence issued by the military court on 14 May 1919.[24] Noske was again presented with Vogel's files on 28 February 1920. The Reich Senior Prosecutor informed him that he had nothing to add to his previous assessment.[25]

As of 26 February, the Dutch government had still not responded. The German Legation sent them another reminder on 10 March 1920,[26] but by then it was too late. For on 8 March, Noske – completely unexpectedly and in violation of all legal assessments, against the Cabinet's

23 BA-Berlin, AA-Vogel, no. 27402/1, 30, letter from the Reich Chancellery to Foreign Office dated 24 January 1920.

24 BA-Berlin, AA-Vogel, no. 27402/1, 134ff.

25 BA-MA, PH 8V/vol. 8, 165R.

26 BA-Berlin, AA-Vogel, no. 27402/1, 143, letter from Rosen to Foreign Office dated 10 March 1920.

decision and his own decree from 26 October 1919 – confirmed Vogel's preposterous sentence.[27]

Noske's behaviour proved that he was not at all interested in solving the case. More than anything, he sought to avoid any further testimony from Vogel, in case he told the truth and shone light into the darkness.

The extradition request was withdrawn on 13 March 1920 (the day the Kapp Putsch began), given that the relatively minor crimes of which Vogel had been convicted by the 'Eden judiciary' were insufficient to justify an extradition.[28] Following the failure of the putsch, the new Chancellor of the Reich, Hermann Müller, sent a baffled letter of enquiry to the Reich Ministry of Defence: 'Herr Chancellor of the Reich would be thankful for an obliging disclosure concerning the reasons which led to the changed decision.'[29] Noske, however, could no longer answer, as he had been forced to step down under pressure from the trade unions and the SPD.

The new minister of defence, Geßler, responded dryly on 6 June 1920: 'For what reasons he [Noske] neglected to further pursue the decision of the Reich Ministry from 7 October 1919 eludes the realm of earthly knowledge.'[30]

---

27   BA-MA, PH 8V/vol. 8, 164.

28   BA-MA, PH 8V/vol. 8, 164; BA-Berlin, AA-Vogel, no. 27402/1, 144 and 148. See also BA-Koblenz, R 43 I 2676, 141, letter from Foreign Office to Reich Chancellery dated 30 April 1920. Hagen Schulze recounts this occurrence in a truncated and thus misleading manner, saying that Vogel was not extradited by the Dutch because the crimes for which he had been sentenced were not extraditable offences; see Schulze, *Kabinett Scheidemann*, 405, n. 11.

29   BA-Koblenz, R 43 I 2676, 142f, letter from Reich Chancellery to the Reich Ministry of Defence dated 12 May 1920.

30   BA-Koblenz, R 43 I 2676, 144, letter from Geßler to Reich Chancellery dated 6 June 1920. Dr Otto Geßler (1875–1955), DDP, Reich

Otto Geßler inspecting an honour guard with Friedrich Ebert on 'Constitution Day', 11 August 1924.

Noske, by contrast, decided to spread a bare-faced lie in his unearthly book, *Von Kiel bis Kapp*: 'I confirmed the sentence reached in the trial for the murders of Liebknecht and Rosa Luxemburg as supreme commander, after the first authorities of the civil and military justice system provided assessments that a repeat of the evidentiary hearing could not be expected to lead to harsher sentences for any of the accused.'[31] The 'first authorities' probably did not read this book, or if they did, no doubt decided to conceal the truth in order to avoid snubbing Herr Noske. Thus Noske deliberately made it impossible to pursue the perpetrators, and created an unconquerable legal bulwark which could be

---

Minister of Defence from 1920 to 1928. Imprisoned in a concentration camp 1944–45. Later served as chairman of the German Red Cross. Coincidentally, Geßler died in the year and place of the author's birth.

31   Noske, *Kiel bis Kapp*, 76.

repeatedly cited, like a kind of legal prayer wheel: the investigation had been concluded in proper fashion and proven nothing. This had the logical consequence of ensuring that future conflicts concerning the individual and collective responsibility for the deed would inevitably meet this legal dead-end. One could almost get the impression that Noske wanted the real perpetrators to go free, in order to avoid kicking up more dust in another trial.

It seems that Noske was afraid the truth could still emerge. A truth which could have damaged him, as well – for if Vogel spilled the beans, he would identify the commander and puppet master lurking in the background, namely Waldemar Pabst. Pabst's arrest would have been tricky but inevitable, and then he probably would have told his side of the story. He did, in fact, state in 1969: 'Even then it was a disgrace that this trial, which neither Ebert nor Noske wanted, had taken place. Noske in particular had promised me that it would not come to that.'[32]

Apropos disgrace: the sluice-gate attendant, Gottfried Knepel, never received the 10,000 marks for discovering Rosa Luxemburg's body that were advertised by the GKSD on its Wanted posters.

---

[32] See document VI, p. 195. Incidentally, concerning a similar trial against First Lieutenant Marloh who ordered thirty sailors killed in March 1919 and was later acquitted, Noske wrote that he considered the trial 'unnecessary in the interests of the state'. Noske, *Erlebtes*, 95.

11

The Seventh Man

Numerous self-incriminating statements had already been given in Luxemburg's case,[1] but on 13 May 1921 State Prosecutor Ortmann was sure he had found the right man: Lieutenant Ernst Krull. 'Krull is strongly suspected of being the as yet unidentified military person who, following the departure of the automobile of Frau Luxemburg from the Hotel Eden, jumped onto the footboard, rode along for a distance, and during the trip fired a shot at Frau Luxemburg before jumping from the automobile.'[2]

Krull's arrest went back to an incident Paul Levi described to the state prosecution: a man had appeared in the offices of the *Rote Fahne* and attempted to sell Rosa Luxemburg's gold watch, claiming to have received it from Lieutenant Krull.[3] The man would subsequently reveal that 'Krull

---

1   For example: BA-Berlin, AA-Vogel, no. 27402/1, 120.

2   BA-Berlin, AA-Vogel, no. 27402/1, 120R.

3   LAB, Rep. 58, no. 75, 1, 59ff, letter from Levi to the state prosecutor dated 28 February 1921.

bragged repeatedly about mur-
dering Luxemburg'.[4] Questioned
by authorities, Krull claimed to
have stolen the watch, as well as
Rosa Luxemburg's school-leaving
certificate and other items, during
a 'house search' of her apartment
one week before her murder.[5] He
also admitted to being the footboard rider on 15 January 1919.
He knew nothing, however, about
the gunshot.

Retired Lieutenant Ernst Krull,
member of the terrorist organi-
sation Consul (OC) and a
spy for the secret police.

Ortmann led the renewed interrogation of the five men
who had accompanied Luxemburg's transport together
with Vogel and the unknown individual. These men were
Poppe, Hall, Grantke, Janschkow, and Weber.[6] The results
of the interrogation? None of them had seen Krull.[7] This
led to the obvious conclusion that Krull, a member of the
Freikorps Rossbach and already convicted in a variety of
fraud cases, had perhaps stolen the watch, but had nothing
to do with Luxemburg's transport. He was indeed a 'footboard passenger' – German slang for a copycat – but only
in the figurative sense. Nevertheless, several pieces of
information obtained in the state prosecutor's further investigations managed to reach the public ear, stoking further

4   Ibid.
5   LAB, Rep. 58, no. 75, 1, 202.
6   BA-Berlin, AA-Vogel, no. 27402/1, 120/121, see also LAB, Rep. 58,
no. 75, vol. 2, 13.
7   BA-Berlin, AA-Vogel, no. 27402/1, 126, letter from Ortmann to the
Reich Ministry of Justice dated 8 December 1921.

speculation: *Rote Fahne* in particular declared Krull to be the murderer and repeated this accusation many times, so that he would go down (falsely) as an accessory to the crime in both East German and Soviet historiography.[8]

But who was this seventh man? Was he a phantom invented by the GKSD to protect Vogel from the murder charge, or did he exist? Some insight can be garnered from an article published in the 28 May 1919 issue of *Die Freiheit*, in which it was reported that court-martial officer Spatz shared 'the regrettable fate of his colleague Jörns [*sic*], as he allegedly was also unaware of what everyone in the Hotel Eden knows, namely that the great Unknown who stood on the automobile is Lieutenant Souchon, who appeared in the trial as a witness.'[9]

The *Berliner Volkszeitung* and the *Vorwärts* repeated this information on the same day. Noske and the highest authorities of the military court as well as the Reich Ministry of Justice remained unaware of the report, which was published at a high print run and with a 'grand layout'.[10] It was not however missed by Kriegsgerichtsrat Spatz, who immediately issued a denial.[11]

The GKSD claimed to know nothing of the accusation levelled against Lieutenant Souchon. Yet *Die Freiheit* had not 'accused' him of anything, merely identified him as the unknown man. Spatz was thus forced to bring the young lieutenant to Berlin as a witness. At that time Souchon was

---

8   See the introduction.
9   *Die Freiheit* 255, 28 May 1919.
10 Schulze, *Kabinett Scheidemann*, 386, n. 2.
11 Reprinted in *Die Freiheit* 257, 29 May 1919.

with the Assault Battalion Schmidt, as an athletics officer in Zossen. Having more important things to attend to in Berlin than appear before the court of his former division – such as purchase athletics equipment[12] – he skipped the appointment. Shortly afterwards he boarded a train to Wilhelmshaven, following the call of the naval base and leaving this rather obnoxious matter behind him.[13]

Souchon had likely witnessed the arrival of Rosa Luxemburg's remains in the Zossen detention centre on 31 May, after Noske ordered them sent there.[14] Perhaps he (or one of his comrades) even managed to visit the corpse before its departure and remove traces of evidence. In a situation where the victim of a murder is housed in the same quarters as the individual suspected of committing it, anything seems possible.

Yet the naval lieutenant did not find peace even after his escape. The driver of Luxemburg's vehicle, Janschkow, would give important testimony in the 1922 investigation of Krull: 'The Krull presented to me is, I can say with certainty, not the person with whom I spoke on other days. That was a Herr in naval uniform; Souchon, as I later heard. When I met him on another day [16 January 1919], Souchon told me he had been there. In what way he was involved I cannot say… As I already testified, the gunshot was fired from behind me on the left. It could well have

---

12   BA-MA, PH 8V/vol. 20, 63, message from Commandant Schmidt dated 6 June 1919.

13   Ibid.

14   According to a letter from Commandant Schmidt dated 20 June 1921, he was in Zossen as late as July 1919, LAB, Rep. 58, No.464, vol. 2, 5.

been fired by the man standing on the left footboard. I cannot say who was standing there.'[15]

State prosecutor Ortmann then ordered that Souchon be interrogated.[16] Souchon, who until then had only been noticed for his modest appearance in the Luxemburg trial, where he was made the crown witness for the officers' 'innocence' by defence lawyer Grünspach,[17] could not be located at first.[18] When he realized he was being searched for in February 1922, he announced from Helsinki: 'Should there be a concern, I am available for a response.'[19] Scandinavia – a popular holiday destination for men of patriotic disposition at the time – had, it would seem, also become a refuge for the retired first lieutenant, who now earned his bread as a bank clerk. Shortly thereafter, he reported that he would return to Germany in May 1923. The state prosecutor planned to subject him to a hearing at this time.[20] Yet in May 1923 'his disposition had undergone a change',[21] and he now planned to stay in Finland. Only then was a pre-trial investigation against him opened, on charges of being an accomplice in the murder of Rosa Luxemburg.[22] His father-in-law would report in the fall of 1923 that Souchon was forced to renounce his visits to

15   LAB, Rep. 58, no. 75, vol. 2, 122f, as well as LAB, Rep. 58, no. 464, vol. 1, 1; Janschkow's trial testimony in BA-MA, PH 8V/vol. 15, 743f.

16   LAB, Rep. 58, no. 75, vol. 2, 126, 13 October 1921.

17   BA-MA, PH 8V/vol. 17, 1010f.

18   LAB, Rep. 58, no. 464, vol. 1, 3ff.

19   Letter from Souchon dated 14 March 1922, ibid., 22.

20   Letter from Souchon dated 29 March 1922, ibid., 23 and statement delivered by state prosecutor Ebelt, 25.

21   Letter from Souchon dated 18 May 1923, ibid., 28.

22   Ibid., 30, see also 26.

Germany altogether, as he was indispensable in Finland.[23] It was by pure chance that a government councillor to the state prosecutor discovered in June 1925 (!) that Souchon was residing in Berlin. He was interrogated the next day.[24]

The young man would state that 'at the time of the matter in question' – meaning the night of 15 January 1919 – he belonged to a naval company under the command of Kaleu von Pflugk-Harttung. They had often 'been called on for special missions' by the GKSD. On the day concerned, he received an order from 'Kaleu' to come to the Hotel Eden with three others (Ritgen, Schulze and Stiege). There, he received the order to convey Dr Liebknecht off the premises. 'When we brought Dr Liebknecht out, I was the last one. Due to the large crowd of people and the automobile's rapid departure it was not possible for me to step into the vehicle, I remained behind.'

Reporting back, he received orders to take part in the later transfer of Frau Luxemburg, and to guard her until then. 'I then did this as well. I was alone in the room with Frau Luxemburg, who read a book.' His watch lasted a little over an hour, he said. Luxemburg was then ordered to get ready. Vogel, appointed leader of the transport team, appeared ten minutes later and 'picked Frau Luxemburg up'. Souchon, Vogel and the non-commissioned officers went out through the revolving doors downstairs. Runge immediately leaped at Frau Luxemburg 'and hit her with the rifle butt while making insulting comments. Vogel, who had

---

23   Letter dated 29 September 1923, ibid., 35.
24   The following quotations are taken from LAB, Rep. 58, no. 464, *Halbakte*, 2ff and vol. 1, 4550.

just gone through the door, quickly jumped between them, then I as well. Runge tried to get to Frau Luxemburg again but backed off in the face of our energetic intervention. Frau Luxemburg was evidently somewhat stunned.' Rosa Luxemburg was then placed in the four-person vehicle.

Souchon submitted a sketch, placing Vogel inside the vehicle, not on the footboard. He forgot infantryman Poppe, who had stood on the left footboard. The two men leaning on the backrest (Vogel and Souchon) as sketched by Souchon had not been seen by any witnesses.

He turned to face the direction of travel and, after only several metres, heard a gunshot next to him. 'I turned

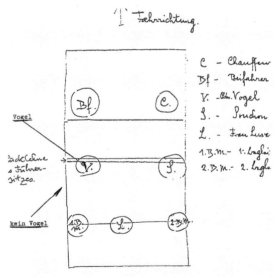

Souchon's sketch

around and saw Frau Luxemburg toppled over backwards; Vogel had a pistol in his hand, the Luger.' Souchon was nevertheless unable to say who fired the shot. He went on to say that he wore a soldier's uniform and had ridden along until the Landwehr Canal. But he stayed in the car, on Vogel's orders. 'Afterwards I heard from the returning soldiers that the body had been thrown into the canal on Vogel's orders. Then we drove back to the Hotel Eden.'

He explained the claim he made during the main trial in 1919, that he had gone home after Liebknecht's transport, by stating that no one ever asked him about the 'Luxemburg affair'. Nor did he seem bothered by the fact that he lied during his interrogation in March 1919, stating that he had seen nothing of Frau Luxemburg's transport.[25] Amazingly, the state prosecutor did not seem to care either. Souchon was dismissed, and boarded a steamship back to Finland the next day. Prosecuting him for perjury did not seem to occur to the state's investigators – at least, no one was prepared to place him under preliminary arrest on such grounds. While Souchon went back to his job as a bank clerk in Finland, the state prosecutor continued with the investigation for years to come. It was only in late October 1925 that anyone thought to expand the proceedings for accessory to murder to include perjury.[26] Thus Souchon would have to be interrogated again, supposedly towards the end of 1925.

---

25   BA-MA, PH 8V/vol. 3, 174R, Souchon's false testimony given on 29 March 1919. See also BA-MA, PH 8V/vol. 13, 221–9, Souchon's false testimony before the field court martial of the GKSD on 9 May 1919. On Souchon's late arrival see BA-MA, PH 8V/vol. 12, 2 and vol. 13, 221.

26   BA-MA, PH 8V/vol. 3, 175, Souchon's testimony dated 29 March 1919.

The suspect responded that although the matter had already been clarified, he was of course prepared to subject himself to a further interrogation, and would let authorities know the next time he was in Germany.[27] After waiting in vain for such a notification, the state prosecutor ultimately closed the investigation on 18 July 1932 (!). Even the judge at the Stuttgart district court, sympathetic to Souchon, was compelled to conclude in 1970 that the proceedings had been conducted 'carelessly' by the state prosecutor at the time.[28] Souchon, by the way, would stay in Berlin now and then, such as in January 1932 when he sought to visit the esteemed Herr 'Major Pabst' for the sake of an 'exchange of thoughts'. As a sympathizer with Finland's fascist Lapua Movement, he had hoped to discuss the possibility of creating a Fascist International. Perhaps the purchase of sports equipment prevented him from visiting the state prosecutor, as had been the case in June 1919.[29]

Even during the hearing before the field court martial, convened by the GKSD in May 1919, no one noticed what would be discovered decades later in the course of the hearing of Süddeutscher Rundfunk, Hans Bausch, and Dieter Ertel: Souchon had arrived 'too late' on the first day of the trial (8 May 1919). In this way he avoided encountering the witnesses to Luxemburg's transport, who perhaps could have identified him as a 'participant'.

---

27   Letter from Souchon dated 16 December 1925, LAB, Rep. 58, No.464, Vol. II, 21.

28   LAB, Rep. 58, No.464, Vol. II, 1 dated 23 October 1925 and 20. Statement given by the Stuttgart judge in *Dokumentation SDR*, 1040.

29   Ibid., 37. See Souchon's letters to Pabst on 18 January and 1 March 1932, BA-SAPMO, NL 35/6, 2022.

```
                    Zeuge Leutnant S o u c h o n.
        -------------------------------------------

Leutnant Hermann S o u c h o n, 24 Jahre alt, evangelisch,
mit keinem der Angeklagten verwandt oder verschwägert.Wegen
Verletzung der Eidespflicht nicht vorbestraft.


Verhandlungsleiter KGR. E h r h a r d t :
     Sie waren gestern um 9 Uhr nicht hier.

Zeuge Leutnant S o u c h o n:
     Nein,ich bin erst später hier gewesen.Es wurde mir gesagt,
dass die Zeugen um 9 Uhr heute morgen herbestellt seien..

Verhandlungsleiter KGR. E h r h a r d t:
     Warum haben Sie sich gestern nicht gemeldet? Ich muss
verlangen,dass Sie,wenn Sie vom Gericht geladen sind,auch
pünktlich um 9 Uhr erscheinen.Veranlassen Sie,dass eine Mel-
dung zu den Akten beigebracht wird,dass Sie verhindert gewesen
seien,pünktlich zu erscheinen.

Zeuge Leutnant S o u c h o n:
     Ich muss jeden Morgen von Zossen hierher kommen.
```

Excerpt from the minutes of the sham trial held before the GKSD field court martial on 9 May 1919.

We can thus conclude that the hearing in June 1925 confirmed (though the public was not apprised of the fact) what *Die Freiheit* wrote on 28 May 1919: the unidentified naval officer, who had in fact 'been along' for the ride, was named Hermann Wilhelm Souchon. This was the seventh man.

12
A Visit from On High

Thirty years after Souchon's hearing, in 1955, Waldemar Pabst returned to the country now known as West Germany. Although he continued to fear the possibility of being kidnapped by East German commandos, he felt increasingly secure as time went on. So secure, in fact, that he began to talk – at least quietly. On 30 November 1959, Pabst's doorbell rang: it was the vice-director of the Federal Office for the Protection of the Constitution, Günther Nollau.

Günther Nollau (1911–1991), President of the Federal Office for the Protection of the Constitution in 1972, photographed here during a discussion with the author on 13 December 1989.

Nollau was visiting, however, not because Pabst was being monitored by his department, but because Nollau wanted to get rid of the headache caused by constant attacks from the East German media concerning then-Federal President Heinrich Lübke's Nazi past.[1] Nollau still remembered the decades-old rumours surrounding the role of Wilhelm Pieck (now the president of East Germany) in the arrest of Luxemburg and Liebknecht, and was seeking ammunition for a counterattack.[2]

Waldemar Pabst struck him as the best source for such ammunition, and Pabst was happy to oblige. He explained to Nollau that Pieck had not betrayed Luxemburg and Liebknecht – he had, after all, been arrested with them – but he did inform on other Communist leaders, and so on. While Nollau immediately published this information in a book,[3] he kept another piece of information to himself, at Pabst's request, and instead – being the intelligence services man he was – recorded a confidential note in his files.[4] He wrote: 'The role of playing the furious mob was reserved for Naval Lieutenant Souchon, who waited for the vehicle carrying Luxemburg at a pre-agreed location. The vehicle stopped, and Souchon fired at the still unconscious

1   Personal account given by Günther Nollau on 13 December 1989. Wilhelm Pieck served as president of the German Democratic Republic from 1949 to 1960.

2   In 1951, Erich Wollenberg described an investigation into Pieck initiated by Hans Kippenberger on Ernst Thälmann's orders in 1931; see, for example, Erich Wollenberg, *Der Apparat*, Bonn: Bundesministerium für gesamtdeutsche Fragen, 1951, 17, n. 3. That such material still exists or rather once existed seems unlikely. At any rate, I was unable to find any trace in the SAPMO archives.

3   Günther Nollau, *International Communism and World Revolution*, New York: Praeger, 1961, 332f.

4   Personal testimony given by Nollau; see also Nollau's testimony before the Stuttgart district court, in *Dokumentation SDR*, 843ff, as well as *Der Spiegel* (1), 1970.

Luxemburg. Luxemburg's corpse was then thrown into the Landwehr Canal. Until now, a First Lieutenant Vogel has always been regarded as the shooter, but this is, according to Pabst's depiction, false.'

First, let us address the accusation concerning Wilhelm Pieck: Pieck spoke about his arrest in numerous statements, letters and interviews. These accounts differ from one another only in terms of minor details.[5]

He was brought to the Hotel Eden together with Luxemburg. While Pabst interrogated Luxemburg in the 'conference room', he was 'watched' by Runge as he stood against the wall in a corner of the hotel.[6] He heard both Liebknecht and Luxemburg being taken away. Then, an officer (probably Petri) came, whispered something to Runge and left. Fearing he might be shot, Pieck turned around, approached Runge and said he wanted to speak with Pabst, whose conference room (meaning the Little Salon) lay directly opposite.

Runge would confirm this in the first Jorns trial: Pieck approached him and said: 'Don't shoot, I haven't been interrogated yet.' While leaving the room, an officer ordered to

---

5   See, among others, Pieck's testimony in the first Jorns trial, LAB, Rep. 58, no. 59, vol. 1, 29k–o. Wilhelm Pieck, 'Der Mord an Rosa Luxemburg und Karl Liebknecht', *Rote Fahne* 11, 13 January 1929. Interview with Wilhelm Pieck in *Rote Fahne*, 15 January 1933, in BA-SAPMO, *Nachlass Pieck*, NL 36/405, 14ff. Wilhelm Pieck, 'Der schwärzteste Tag', in BA-SAPMO, I 2/711/46, Juristische Zentralstelle, 48ff. Wilhelm Pieck, 'Der Mord an Rosa Luxemburg und Karl Liebknecht', in ibid., 40ff. Wilhelm Pieck, 'Die Ermordung von Rosa Luxemburg und Karl Liebknecht', *Inprekorr*, 10 January 1928, in BA-SAPMO, NL 1/19, 7678. Wilhelm Pieck, 'Mit dem Leben davongekommen', 6 February 1953, in ibid., 97f.

6   See construction plans for the Hotel Eden.

have him taken away: 'And it's your responsibility to make sure that nothing happens.'[7]

Pieck indicated that he went to Pabst, managed to deceive him as to his identity and was eventually brought to the police station. He escaped in the courtyard by convincing one of his guards, who sympathized with the Communists, to let him go.[8] The fact is that Pabst had no idea at the time of who Pieck was. He did not even know his name,[9] and presumed him to be an editor of the *Rote Fahne*.

It is conceivable that Runge, acting under Captain Petri's orders, wanted to shoot Pieck. For Pabst, however, such an execution would have constituted a *'coram publico'* – not to mention been simply foolish, particularly right in front of his office.[10] Moreover, Pabst had no interest in having Pieck shot, as the man seemed far too insignificant.[11]

Pabst clearly exaggerated when claiming that Pieck had betrayed 'military information'; he was imposing his soldier's mentality onto the protagonists of the Spartacus League. Pieck, an absolute amateur when it came to military and insurrectionary matters, could not have revealed anything concerning the Spartacus League's military organization, as no such thing existed. Nor could he betray the location of important 'Spartacus leaders': Luxemburg and Liebknecht were already dead, Leo Jogiches[12] and Georg

---

7   BA-MA, PH 8V/vol. 8, 125, Runge's testimony in the first Jorns trial as reported in the *Rote Fahne*, 23 April 1929.

8   Pieck's testimony in the first Jorns trial stated rather dryly: 'where I managed to escape', LAB, Rep. 58, no. 59, vol. 1, 29m.

9   Pabst's account in: BA-MA, PH 8V/vol. 13, 201.

10   See document II in the appendix to this volume.

11   Ibid.

12   Jacob, 'Krieg und Revolution', 497.

Ledebour sat in prison,[13] and Karl Radek would not be arrested until February.[14]

Pieck would make his final comments on the matter, which was visibly embarrassing to him, in 1953. This time, he complained that the Western press was using Pabst's alleged memoirs to shamelessly libel him. Pabst had already emitted an order to shoot him at the time (15 January 1919), but he (Pieck) managed to fool him by claiming to be an editor of the *Frankfurter Zeitung*. This story does not sound particularly believable.

It is certainly possible that Pieck, fearing for his life, betrayed the addresses of his comrades or perhaps merely gave false information, given that Pabst would not retract this claim – even in private correspondence with his comrade-in-murder, von Pflugk-Harttung, in the 1960s.[15]

---

13 Ledebour's testimony in the second Jorns trial as reported in the *Berliner Tageblatt*, 6 February 1930.

14 Otto Ernst Schüddekopf, 'Karl Radek in Berlin', *Archiv für Sozialgeschichte*, II, 1962, 'Anlage 1: Bericht über Radeks Verhaftung', 109ff. The arrest warrant, however, was dated 16 January 1919, ibid., 91.

15 Letter from Pabst to Pflugk-Harttung dated 14 July 1962, BA-MA, N 620/36.

13

The Confession

Two years after Nollau's visit, in late 1961, Pabst was angered by an article published by Gerhard Zwerenz in the news magazine *Stern*,[1] and decided to launch a counterattack. In his own publication, *Das deutsche Wort*,[2] he openly admitted, for the first time, to giving the order to kill: 'This decision to eliminate the two pernicious and docile pupils of Moscow was not easy for me.' The article was swiftly reprinted in other nationalist journals, including the *Stahlhelm* and the *Deutscher Studentenanzeiger*.

The West German government, with whose press office Pabst was on excellent terms (probably through his old comrade-in-arms Albrecht Freiherr von Wechmar), issued an (in)famous communiqué labelling the double homicide a 'legitimate execution'.[3] Pabst felt officially vindicated at last.

---

1 *Stern* 47, 16 November 1961.

2 *Das deutsche Wort* 1, 5 January 1962.

3 Bulletin of the Press and Information Service of the German Federal Government, no. 27, 8 February 1962. The decree has not been repealed to this day. Sixteen years earlier, the murder of Luxemburg and Liebknecht was

Pabst during an interview with *Spiegel* editors Hans Schmelz and Martin Virchow in 1962.

Soon afterwards, Pabst granted to *Der Spiegel* the notorious interview in which he claimed to have 'allowed' Luxemburg and Liebknecht 'to be taken care of'.[4]

He added: 'What I discussed with those gentlemen who volunteered for the transports – none of them were ordered to do it – is nobody's business.'[5] Nothing happened, despite furious letters to the editor and multiple lawsuits,[6] other than Pabst temporarily retreating to another part of the country after several threatening phone calls. His prediction that no state prosecutor would be willing to take up 'the idiotic suit brought by the L[iebknecht] widow and the lawyer Dr Arndt' would prove correct.

---

still regarded as a crime against humanity in the same country.

4   *Der Spiegel* 16, 1962, 38. Available online at spiegel.de (last accessed July 2018).

5   Ibid., 43.

6   *Der Spiegel* 18, 1962, 510; *Der Spiegel* 23, 1962, 90. Pabst's assessment can be read in a letter he wrote to Pflugk-Harttung dated 14 July 1962, BA-MA, N 620/36.

Yet because he had broken an old promise, his old comrade-in-murder von Pflugk-Harttung decided to get in touch:[7] he reminded Pabst that he had 'committed' them 'to maintain absolute silence' at the time, and that the same applied to him. Pabst therefore knew that any accomplices who were still alive were less than enthusiastic about his revelations. Yet he continued to blab.

---

7   Letter from Pflugk-Harttung to Pabst dated 3 May 1962, BA-MA, N 620/36.

14
The Assignment

In 1966, German television journalist Dieter Ertel was commissioned to write a docu-drama to mark the fiftieth anniversary of Rosa Luxemburg and Karl Liebknecht's death. Besides studying the court-martial files, he engaged in a lively correspondence with Pabst and made several fruitful visits to him, accompanied by a witness (memory logs of the interviews are documented in the appendix to this volume).

During the first visit Pabst claimed, among other things, that the order to shoot Rosa Luxemburg was given to Lieutenant Souchon. He was to wait at a predetermined point along the route, and there carry out the deed. 'It was to be presented as if an unknown individual among the angry mob had fired the shot.'[1] In light of this interview, Ertel and his witness believed that after the incident with Runge, Vogel had lost his nerve and shot Rosa Luxemburg himself. Ertel received the files of the Krull case a short

---

1   See document I in the appendix to this volume.

Director Theo Metzger, producer Gustav Strübel, and author Dieter Ertel (from left) during the filming of the made-for-TV movie *Der Fall Liebknecht-Luxemburg*, sitting in the car used in the re-enactment of Luxemburg's murder.

while later. The testimony from Janschkow (see chapter eleven) not only indicated that Souchon had been present during the transport, but also that he probably stood on the footboard. Ertel visited Pabst again and put to him his suspicions about Lieutenant Souchon: he had obviously ridden in the automobile. Pabst responded: 'No, he did not join the ride. Souchon jumped on the footboard and shot Rosa Luxemburg from there.'[2]

---

2   See document III in the appendix to this volume.

15
Fifty Years Later

Ertel was eager to incorporate this new piece of information into his television drama, and publicized the fact in a press conference.[1] However, shortly before the drama was to be aired, in December 1968, Souchon – now retired and living in Bad Godesberg – filed a provisional injunction against the broadcaster, the publicly-owned Süddeutscher Rundfunk. The court ruled that the drama in which Souchon was depicted as the shooter could be aired, provided it incorporated a disclaimer stating that it 'did not depict proven, factual claims in all aspects'.[2] What lay behind this decision?

Shortly after Ertel's press conference, Souchon contacted the lawyer Otto Kranzbühler (who had successfully defended Grand Admiral Karl Dönitz and the CEO of Krupp Steel, Friedrich K. Krupp, in the Nuremberg

---

1 See document IV in the appendix to this volume; see also *Der Spiegel* 8, 1967, 40ff.

2 Provisional decision of the Stuttgart district court on 23 December 1968, in *Dokumentation SDR*, 517.

Trials). A shrewd former naval judge himself, who had sported the four stripes of a captain at sea on his uniform, Kranzbühler agreed to take on Souchon's legal representation and paid Pabst a memorable visit. According to Kranzbühler, Pabst related a few details of his struggle against the 'November Revolution'[3] before suddenly blurting out: 'Between the two of us, of course I gave Souchon the order to shoot Rosa Luxemburg – and he shot her.'[4]

Otto Kranzbühler as Dönitz's defence lawyer before the International Military Tribunal during the Nuremburg trials in 1946.

Kranzbühler then presented Pabst with a sworn affidavit from Souchon, in which he affirmed: 'I did not fire at Rosa Luxemburg.'[5]

Pabst blanched on reading Souchon's statement,[6] doubtless realizing that this comrade-in-arms was not particularly keen to play along and had no intention of corroborating Pabst's confession. To avoid leaving his former comrade high and dry, Pabst backpedalled somewhat and signed a sworn affidavit for Kranzbühler stating that he never told Ertel that Souchon fired the shot.[7]

---

3   See also chapter sixteen, 'Seventy-Four Years Later'.

4   Written note from Herr Kranzbühler dated 10 November 1989.

5   Sworn statement by H. W. Souchon dated 6 December 1968, in *Dokumentation SDR*, 448f.

6   Personal statement by Herr Kranzbühler on 8 January 1990.

7   Sworn statement by Pabst dated 17 December 1968, in *Dokumentation SDR*, 498.

This did not exclude the possibility that Souchon was the shooter, but Ertel had nevertheless lost his most important witness, a plight exacerbated by Pabst's decision not to give any further official statements. Privately, however, Pabst left no doubt as to whom he had given the fateful order on that January night in 1919 to murder Rosa Luxemburg, nor as to what he thought of sworn affidavits: nothing at all.

Shortly after, Pabst wrote to his lawyer that Kranzbühler had 'not understood the matter at all, otherwise he would not have surprised me with the sworn affidavit'. Pabst was caught in a dilemma: Vogel or Souchon. Counting in Souchon's favour was 'his volunteering to commit the deed or, if you will, to execute it according to my orders'. He had involved other comrades as little as possible. Pabst had kept Souchon out of the whole thing for forty years for this very reason, but since it was now a question of elucidating what really happened, he had named him (to Ertel). He should have named him as soon as the Süddeutscher Rundfunk launched its series (the docu-drama was part of a series titled *Befangene Justiz*, or 'biased judiciary'). Addressing Ertel, Pabst noted: 'Herr Souchon explained in his defence that "I", his superior at the time, "was an unreliable adventurer". But then why did he volunteer for the task on the orders of an "adventurer"? To liquidate Frau L.?' Pabst also speaks of 'Herr Souchon and the predicament caused by his fairy tale', describing his former comrade as dishonest.[8]

---

8 Quotations taken from previously undiscovered writings by Pabst, in BA-MA, N 620/21, in Pabst's handwriting, on stationery with his Lucerne address, to his lawyer Dr Max Bürger in early January 1969; BA-MA, N 620/46, draft of a letter to Dieter Ertel (January 1969), in Pabst's handwriting, marked 'material'; BA-MA, N 620/21, draft of a letter to Ertel dated

Yet this was of little help to Ertel, as no one else would see Pabst's written remarks. Although the drama was shown in two parts on 14 and 15 January 1969 by Germany's central public broadcaster, ARD, Souchon had already been given the chance to seize the initiative.

And seize it he did. Two months after the broadcast, he filed a suit against Süddeutscher Rundfunk, its director Hans Bausch, and the writer Dieter Ertel. Negotiations between the parties were conducted in 1969 and 1970.

Pabst, who was already very ill at this point, could not or rather would not undergo another hearing.

Martin Benrath as Waldemar Pabst, Edith Heerdegen as Rosa Luxemburg in the SDR made-for-TV movie. Pabst wrote to Franz von Papen in 1968: 'I am curious to see how Benrath portrays me. Wechmar was excited and claimed that sometimes he could not tell whether he was looking at me, his old boss, or an actor.'

Nevertheless, hitherto unknown handwritten notes by Pabst from the time spell things out very clearly. Even then, Pabst was quite certain of who had committed the deed: Souchon.[9]

The general public, however, were not told about this. Instead, they were treated to the peculiar spectacle of a trial seeking to determine who really fired the shot – fifty years after Rosa Luxemburg's murder – in the absence of

9 January 1969, typewritten, continued by hand and then abandoned. Pabst omitted this passage in the letter he actually sent, see *Dokumentation SDR*, 195f.

9   Letter from Ertel to Pabst dated 2 January 1969, in: BA-MA, N 620/46. See also Pabst's handwritten marginalia on Ertel's sworn statement given on 19 December 1968, ibid.

in seinem Plädoyer bewertete. Er sagte, man könne unser Fernseh-
spiel "die Hauptmann-Pabst-Story" überschreiben, denn Sie hätten
sich darin von uns als Retter des Vaterlandes in entscheidender
Stunde feiern lassen. Herr Dr. Karch wollte damit anscheinend
artikulieren, daß wir uns bei unserer Arbeit allzu sehr von
Ihnen und Ihrer Darstellung der damaligen Ereignisse hätten
beeinflussen lassen, und daß dabei die geschichtliche Wahrheit
in einigen Details - z. B. der Erschießung Rosa Luxemburgs -
unter die Räder gekommen sei.

Lieber Herr Pabst, ich errate und verstehe durchaus die Gründe,
aus denen heraus Sie sich entschlossen haben, in letzter Minute
Herrn Souchon beizuspringen. Aber wenn Ihre Darstellung jetzt
darauf hinausläuft, Sie hätten zwar Herrn Souchon den Befehl
gegeben, Rosa Luxemburg zu exekutieren, wüßten aber nicht, ob
dieser Befehl auch so ausgeführt worden sei, so kann ich Ihnen
nur antworten: Ich war selbst Soldat und weiß, daß über einen
ausgeführten Befehl Vollzugsmeldung zu erstatten ist. Daß man
Sie falsch ins Bild gesetzt hätte und daß ausgerechnet Sie im
Irrtum gewesen wären, als Sie annahmen, Souchon habe geschossen,
das lasse ich mir nun wirklich nicht einreden. Denn eines geht
ja nun aus meinen Forschungen wirklich zweifelsfrei hervor: nämlich
daß Sie - späterdann auch Canaris - sämtliche Fäden in der Hand
hatten und über nichts im unklaren geblieben sind. Nur so war
ja auch die geradezu raffinierte Prozeßregie möglich.

Ich möchte Sie über das alles doch ehrlich informiert haben,
obwohl ich es heute fast für unwahrscheinlich halte, daß der
Rechtsstreit noch weitergeht. Immerhin haben wir ja unser Haupt-
ziel erreicht, nämlich die Sendung ausstrahlen zu dürfen. Und
was Herrn Souchon betrifft, so hat er eine eidesstattliche Ver-
sicherung abgegeben, die für mich als Kenner der Materie von
Ungereimtheiten und haarsträubenden Widersprüchen nur so strotzt.
Außerdem hat er - dies ist natürlich mein privater Eindruck -
bei seinen Aussagen vor dem Stuttgarter Landgericht einen Eindruck gemacht, der alles andere als überzeugend war, um mich
milde auszudrücken. Er wäre wirklich gut beraten, wenn er sich
wieder in den Hintergrund verzöge, in dem er sich 50 Jahre lang
aufgehalten hat; auch das ist natürlich meine private Meinung.

Die Bilanz: Wir haben mit unserer unglückseligen Pressekonferenz
einen Fehler gemacht. Niemand hat mehr Grund, das zu beklagen als
ich. Ich nehme mir aber die Freiheit hinzuzufügen: Ich glaube,
Sie haben auch einen Fehler gemacht. Wir saßen in einem Boot. Und
daß Sie dabei nicht schlecht gefahren sind, zeigt nichts besser
als die Reaktion von Souchons Anwalt ("Retter des Vaterlandes" usw.).

Mit den besten Grüßen, auch an Ihre verehrte Frau Gemahlin,

Ihr sehr ergebener

(Dieter Ertel)

Ertel's letter to Pabst from January 1969. Ertel writes: 'I myself was a soldier, and
know that the implementation of an order is to be reported.' Pabst's handwritten
note in the margins reads: 'I received the implementation report verbally from Hr.
Vogel, S.[ouchon] fired the shot.' Further below: 'The deed occurred on m.[y]
orders, n.[ot] without the knowledge of higher authorities.'

the key witness, Waldemar Pabst. Even more bizarre was the fact that the man accused of the murder appeared as the plaintiff, while the man who revealed his actions sat in the dock. Just imagine, to take a more recent example from the 1990s, if the former director of the East German Ministry for State Security, Erich Mielke, had not been prosecuted, but instead was allowed to sue everyone who accused him of the murder of two police officers back in 1931.

But let us return to the case of *Souchon v. Ertel, Bausch and the SDR*. Citing a lack of eyewitnesses – and it was this fact that made the trial so shameful – the Stuttgart district court proceeded in 1969–70, based on an examination of the records. The judge treated the records of the GKSD's court martial like any others: he assumed them to be true and accurate. Jorns's lies, his efforts to conceal the crime, the observing Council members' decision to withdraw, the trial by fellow officers, the Canaris case – none of it seemed to carry any weight for this judge. All that counted were the files and the testimony of that 'respectable officer of Prussian stock', Souchon.[10]

Doubt was cast on the notion of an officers' plot, and Pabst's underlying role was disregarded, as unproven. Almost all the admissions made by Pabst since his return to West Germany were dismissed for want of credibility. The affair more resembled 'the methods of a disingenuous slanderer';[11] Pabst was regarded overall as an inadmissible and unreliable witness.

---

10   Verdict of the Stuttgart district court on 12 February 1970, 135, in *Dokumentation SDR*, 1079.

11   Ibid., 160, in *Dokumentation SDR*, 1104.

The perpetrator as plaintiff: Hermann W. Souchon before the Stuttgart district court, taken from the pages of *Stern* magazine, no. 8, 1969.

Without the slightest proof, the judge claimed that Pabst had suffered from cerebral sclerosis since at least 1959.[12] Süddeutscher Rundfunk and Ertel were ordered to retract their claims (on the country's most-watched news programme, the *Tagesschau*, no less!).

A challenge to the partisan judge on grounds of bias filed by the director of Süddeutscher Rundfunk, Dr Bausch (a Christian Democrat), was roundly rejected.[13]

Ertel, the SDR and Bausch then lodged an appeal. Yet the judges from the district court of appeals proved

12   Ibid., 118, in *Dokumentation SDR*, 1062.
13   See *Dokumentation SDR*, 904–43.

equally overwhelmed by the level of historical complexity involved. They did not even attempt to weigh up the trade-offs between the rights of the individual and the right to freedom of expression in the trial, but accepted the court records at face value and felt very secure in this decision.[14]

Because the three men who had accompanied the murder vehicle – Poppe, Weber, and Grantke – claimed that Vogel fired the shot, it must have been Vogel. These three were believed, while Janschkow and Hall, the two drivers who claimed the contrary, were arbitrarily written off as liars. The possibility that Weber, Grantke and Poppe had been bribed, as had been the case with Runge and the drivers, was ruled out, and Poppe's suggestion that pressure had been exerted was ignored as trivial.

Recorded exchange during the main trial on 12 May 1919:

WITNESS POPPE: Yes, I was asked to say everything in this fashion.

...

CHIEF NEGOTIATOR KRIEGSGERICHTSRAT EHRHARDT: Do you mean by that, that you were influenced from any quarter during your interrogation?

WITNESS POPPE: I was so weak-willed at that point.

REPRESENTATIVE OF THE PROSECUTION KRIEGSGERICHTSRAT JORNS: Just as scared as today.[15]

---

14   See above and n. 41 <c9> .
15   BA-MA, PH 8V/vol. 15, 700, Poppe's testimony.

The fact that the three officers had been put under enormous pressure was disregarded, as was the fact that their testimony kept the unidentified man out of the picture, or that the escape for their named culprit, Vogel, had long been prepared.[16] That Vogel moreover never stood on the footboard where the perpetrator must have stood, according to these men's testimony, proved as unproblematic as the numerous contradictions in Souchon's testimony, in which he sought to portray himself as a mere passenger who had nothing to do with the events.[17]

Even Pabst's letter of 30 May 1967,[18] in which he confirmed Souchon's decision to volunteer for the mission, was dismissed as an unsoluble puzzle. All this could only happen because the gentlemen of the court assumed that Pabst had been suffering from memory loss since 1967 (!), making his statements mere nonsense. Not even the possibility that Souchon might have fired was admitted as evidence.[19] It was refuted by the records of the trial conducted by his fellow soldiers! The result? Souchon was cast as an unknowing, uninvolved passenger, the officers' plot

16   The idea that Weber, who also accused Vogel in the Krull trial, could have still been afraid of the officers in 1921 was unthinkable for the judges. LAB, Rep. 58, no. 75, vol. 2, 41f.

17   Weber's eyewitness testimony before the state prosecutor in 1921: 'If Vogel was sitting in the automobile, then he certainly didn't fire the shot.' See *Dokumentation SDR*, 1242ff, letter from Dieter Ertel dated 30 November 1970.

18   Verdict of the Stuttgart superior district court on 20 January 1971 (henceforth 'Stuttgart superior court verdict'), 76, in *Dokumentation SDR*, 1407. A copy of this verdict can also be found in BA-SAPMO, *Nachlass Luxemburg*, NY 4002/65 (previously NL 2/65), 16–111. See also Pabst's letter to Ertel, document V in the annex to this volume.

19   Stuttgart superior court verdict, 74 and 81, in *Dokumentation SDR*, 1405 and 1412.

hatched in the Hotel Eden was denied, and the murder of Luxemburg and Liebknecht became a curiously synchronized and yet disjointed operation.

Given what we know today, there can be no doubt of either an officers' plot directed by Pabst nor of Souchon's involvement – even without taking Pabst's testimony into account.

1. Souchon was the only member of the naval squadron in 1919 who had not sat in the dock, but rather was interrogated as a passive witness. The reason, besides his false testimony given on 29 March 1919 and his perjury committed at the trial itself (on 1 May 1919), was his claim that he (a giant at 1.90m) had been assigned to Liebknecht's transport but was held back by a large crowd (which did not exist) at the side entrance to the Hotel Eden during Liebknecht's departure, and thus could not join the others.

Souchon claimed in 1919 that he went home after failing to participate in Liebknecht's execution. Beyond the fact that he was genuinely not involved in Liebknecht's transport – that is to say, was not held back by a fictitious crowd – he was portrayed as having been entirely uninvolved, and could thus exonerate his comrades as a naïve witness. The officers' defence lawyer, Grünspach, argued consistently in the 1919 trial that had Pflugk-Harttung truly concocted a murderous plan, he would never have appointed a 'bystander', namely Souchon, as group leader, but rather would have selected the perpetrator himself.[20]

---

20   BA-MA, PH 8V/vol. 17, 1010, remarks by defence lawyer Grünspach.

Yet that Pflugk-Harttung hatched just such a plan is incontrovertibly proven by Ernst von Weizsäcker's diary entry and a letter from Pflugk-Harttung to Pabst.[21] From this, we can conclude – fully in agreement with Grünspach's line of argument – that the man whose job it was to choose the perpetrators must have known what he was getting into, and this man was without a doubt Souchon.

2. Souchon justified his presence in Luxemburg's transport in 1968 as follows: after being held back by the crowd, he reported to Captain Rühle von Lilienstern. Von Lilienstern told Souchon: 'That is convenient, because the transport of Frau Luxemburg, of which First Lieutenant Vogel has been appointed leader, must go ahead immediately; since the accompanying personnel consists entirely of non-commissioned officers, it is advisable that as well as the transport leader, one more officer should go along.'[22]

One cannot but wonder how many officers a transport of this size really required. Surely just one, in this case Vogel, who also wore an officer's uniform. That is, of course, unless the officers had something else in mind. So what about Souchon?

Given that, according to his own statements, he was serving as a regular soldier and wearing the corresponding uniform, the explanation that he was needed as a second officer is simply illogical. Not only was a second officer

---

21   Letter from Pflugk-Harttung to Pabst dated 3 May 1962, BA-MA, N 620/36.

22   Sworn statement by H. W. Souchon on 6 December 1958, in: *Dokumentation SDR*, 448f.

superfluous for the transport, Souchon would not have been recognized as such by the other accompanying soldiers.

3. In the same sworn affidavit from 1968, Souchon explains, as he did in 1919 and 1925, his own activity and that of his fellows: 'Pflugk-Harttung went to receive the orders, while the remaining officers from our group waited.'[23] This had given defence lawyer Grünspach the opportunity to clear Pflugk-Harttung's name in 1919.

Grünspach: 'When they [the men from the naval squadron] entered the Hotel Eden, Lieutenant Commander von Pflugk-Harttung immediately went to the room in which Liebknecht waited and did not leave that room, as is ... proven by the sworn statement of Lieutenant Souchon... He [Pflugk-Harttung] could not therefore have worked out a plan with his officers in the Hotel Eden, nor discussed how to kill Herr Liebknecht.'[24]

But there is a catch: according to both Heinrich Stiege's testimony on 6 December 1967 and Pflugk-Harttung's letter to Pabst dated 3 May 1962, this plan was indeed drafted in the Hotel Eden. Eight months before his death, Stiege was visited by Ertel, who asked how Pabst had given him and the naval officers the order to execute Luxemburg and Liebknecht in the Hotel Eden in 1919. Stiege did not remember the details anymore; he only recalled that 'summary execution' had been discussed. This could not be carried out due to the political situation, however, and would have

23   Ibid.
24   BA-MA, PH 8V/vol. 17, 1011, Grünspach's remarks.

An exact reconstruction: Martin Benrath as Captain Pabst (left) orders the camouflaged naval officers (Helmut Dietl as Souchon, in the middle, and Karl Walter Diess as Kaleu Pflugk-Harttung, on the right) in his general staff office in the Hotel Eden to murder Rosa Luxemburg and Karl Liebknecht. Still photograph taken from the SDR made-for-TV film in 1969.

to be disguised, so that Liebknecht and Luxemburg would not be cast as martyrs.[25]

Moreover, Pflugk-Harttung wrote to Pabst in 1962: 'You had at that time committed us to maintain absolute silence.'[26]

In sum, some kind of agreement was reached in Pabst's room. The naval officers could not have waited on the stairs the whole time, as Souchon insisted until the very end.

This also means that Souchon's claim in the 1969–70 trial, that he had not even seen Pabst in the evening of 15

---

25 Sworn statement by Dieter Ertel on 19 December 1968, in *Dokumentation SDR*, 480. See also Dieter Ertel, 'Einer aus dem Tiergarten', *Der Monat* 20 (243), December 1968, 44.

26 Letter from Pflugk-Harttung to Pabst dated 3 May 1962, BA-MA, N 620/36, points 1 and 2.

January 1919, is patently untrue.[27] It proves that his statements made in 1919, 1925, and from 1968 to 1970 are untrue and devoid of value. Whichever German legal system was dealing with his case at any given time, Souchon lied to all of them – without exception.

And now to Pabst's claims. Until the Stuttgart trials, Pabst had been generally viewed as a trustworthy source on historical events.[28] The conservative historian Johannes Erger was particularly fond of using Pabst's reports. In his standard reference work on the Kapp Putsch, *Der Kapp-Lüttwitz-Putsch*, Pabst's statements are cited as evidence in over fifty footnotes.[29]

Erger first met Pabst as a student, visited him repeatedly and corresponded with him over the years. Pabst told him about the agreement among the officers and the 'summary court martial'.[30] Erger was also present at the first conversation between Pabst and Dieter Ertel. On this, he once said: 'Well, the most extensive, certainly by far the most extensive account and in my view the most trustworthy on all points is contained in this record compiled by Herr Ertel [see documents I–III in the appendix]. According to my recollection, this paper possesses a very high historical value, and in case of doubt, by my estimation, Pabst should sooner be followed than any other.'

---

27   Stuttgart superior court verdict, 57.

28   See *Wirren*, 32–54, 72f, as well as Hagen Schulze's Freikorps anthology: Hagen Schulze, *Freikorps*, 29f, 39, 80, 207, 212ff.

29   Johannes Erger, *Der Kapp-Lüttwitz-Putsch. Ein Beitrag zur deutschen Innenpolitik 1919–20*, Düsseldorf: Droste, 1967.

30   Personal communication from Prof. Dr Johannes Erger dated 11 March 1991.

Both Erger and Nollau utterly discount the notion that Pabst suffered from memory loss. Nollau was also convinced that Souchon had been the perpetrator.[31]

Pabst – who, by the way, never said that Vogel fired the shot – had no reason to accuse the wrong man in the late 1960s. On the contrary: it was his wish, as shown in his extensive correspondence with political associates, that the truth and with it his leading role in this double homicide should finally come to light.

Why else would he have absolved the already deceased Vogel (whom he strongly disliked) and instead pointed the finger at Souchon (whom he liked very much)? Pabst had simply not expected that his comrades would refuse to admit to their deed fifty years later – purely out of fear of moral condemnation, given that legally nothing could happen to them in West Germany (the victims were communists, after all). Pabst, however, was convinced that his action had been necessary. He believed he had saved the Christian West and was proud of it. Accordingly, he had no reason to tell a lie or to shield himself. He knew he would not be prosecuted in West Germany. Furthermore, his claims had always been proven to be essentially credible when cross-checked against other evidence.[32]

His last handwritten notes, which were not intended for the public and were not yet available in the 1970s, leave no

---

31 Personal communication from Günther Nollau dated 13 December 1989.

32 On this, see nos 3 <c2>, 6 <c2>, 2 <c3>, 5 <c3>, 8 <c3>, 20 <c3>, 18 <c4>, 3 <c6>, 7 <c7>, 16 <c7>, 17 <c7>, 20 <c7>, 11 <c8>, 5 <c9>, 12 <c9>, 14 <c9>, 16 <c9>, 17 <c9>, 16 <c14>, 24 <c14>, as well as *Internationale wissenschaftliche Korrespondenz*, 3, 1992, 363f, and document II, p. 179.

trace of doubt: Pabst was convinced to the end of his life that Hermann W. Souchon volunteered to murder Rosa Luxemburg and carried out the deed.[33] Nor did he ever forget to mention that his orders had been approved at the time by 'higher authorities'.[34]

---

33   See document VII in the appendix to this volume.

34   Handwritten note by Pabst in a letter to Dieter Ertel dated 2 January 1969. Pabst kept this comment to himself and did not send it to Ertel. BA-MA, N 620/46.

16
Seventy-Four Years Later

When I first published my findings in an essay in 1992, I sent a copy to Souchon's former lawyer, Otto Kranzbühler. Quite elderly at this point, the man answered promptly and, feeling somewhat pressured by my publication, revealed a secret he had kept carefully hidden until then.

Herr Kranzbühler, a naval judge in the Second World War and successful defender of Admiral Karl Dönitz and Friedrich K. Krupp in the Nuremberg Trials, had a fateful encounter with Waldemar Pabst on 17 December 1968. Herr Kranzbühler had adroitly skirted a certain detail of his discussion with Pabst, both in his 1969 testimony to the Stuttgart district court and in an interview with me in 1990 (telling me: 'That is so fantastical that I would prefer to erase it from my memory'[1]). He brought it up for the first time in his letter: 'Pabst had, as you know [I did not], assured me that he called Noske before making his decision

---

[1] Recorded interview that the author and Martin Choroba conducted with Kranzbühler in Tegernsee, Germany on 6 January 1990.

[to have Luxemburg and Liebknecht murdered on the evening of 15 January 1919]. Noske instructed him to first obtain permission from General von Lüttwitz to execute the two prisoners, and when Pabst exclaimed "I will never get it", responded by saying "Then you will have to take responsibility for what must be done".'[2]

Kranzbühler's statement is the last piece of a puzzle, many pieces of which can be found in Pabst's personal files. In his fragmented memoirs, Pabst wrote down what happened after Luxemburg and Liebknecht's internment in the Hotel Eden:

> Then I went back into my office in order to consider, for the few minutes in which I could have some peace to think, how the execution of those two whom we considered to be deeply guilty traitors to the nation ought to be carried out.
>
> Neither Herr Noske nor I had the slightest doubt that it had to be done as we discussed the need to end the civil war. From Noske's 'insinuations' I could only deduce that he shared my opinion that Germany must settle down as soon as possible... There was thus agreement regarding the 'what'. When I said, Herr Noske, please give me orders concerning the 'how', Noske replied: 'That is not my concern! The party would fall apart, as it is not open to such measures under any circumstances. The General [von Lüttwitz, Pabst's superior] should do it, they're his prisoners.'[3]

In a scrawled note in the margin of a letter from Dieter Ertel, dated 2 January 1969, he wrote: 'The deed was

---

2 Letter from Kranzbühler to the author dated 12 January 1993.
3 Pabst, *Memoirs*, 65f.

done on my orders and not without informing higher authorities, otherwise they hardly would have spared me!! But that is a chapter in itself and does not belong in this trial, nor in the public sphere whatsoever.' (See the facsimile on 127).

Furthermore, in a letter to Dr Georg Franz dated 22 February 1969, Pabst wrote: 'Noske and I were wholly in agreement on this assessment. Of course, Noske could not emit the orders himself.'[4]

Pabst himself recounted

Euch allen, die Ihr vier Jahre lang die deutsche Heimat heldenhaft geschützt habt, gilt in erster Linie dieser Mahnruf. Helft auch jetzt mit, die bitterste Not abzuwenden. Meldet Euch bei den Freiwilligen Verbänden, die die Regierung zum Schutze der Grenzen und zur

Aufrechterhaltung von Sicherheit und Ordnung im Innern

aufgestellt hat.

Pflicht aller Behörden und Privatunternehmer ist es, die Werbung mit allen Mitteln zu unterstützen. Sie müssen im Interesse der großen Sache dafür sorgen, daß die sich freiwillig Meldenden keinen Schaden für ihre dienstliche, geschäftliche und wissenschaftliche Zukunft erleiden.

Der Zentralrat der deutschen sozialistischen Republik gez. Cohen.

Der Oberbefehlshaber der Regierungstruppen in Berlin gez. Noske.

Berliner, meldet Euch sofort bei der **Garde-Kavallerie-Schützen-Division** Berlin, Nürnberger Str. 70 (Deutsches Künstlertheater).

Pabst in 1969: 'Noske was exemplary'.

another variant of Noske's approval at a meeting of veteran military cadets in the mid-1960s. The renowned military historian and retired Lieutenant Colonel Ernst-Heinrich Schmidt listened to the lecture, in which Pabst claimed that he personally informed Noske of Liebknecht and Luxemburg's arrest, and, upon suggesting shooting the two of them, received a nod of the head from Noske (who was hunched over his files). Schmidt described Pabst as disliked, self-involved and egomaniacal but also charismatic and, in this case, absolutely trustworthy.[5]

---

4   BA-MA, N 620/17.
5   Personal communication from Ernst-Heinrich Schmidt, 4 August 2018. The speech to the veterans was recorded on tape.

Pabst responded most vehemently, however, when the Stuttgart district court called on him to give testimony during Souchon's lawsuit against Ertel in June 1969 (see previous chapter). Around this time, he wrote:

The fact is: the execution of the orders given by me ... happened, and these Germans should thank Noske and myself on their knees for it, build monuments to us and name streets and public squares after us! Noske was exemplary, and the party (except for its half-Communist left wing) behaved impeccably in this affair. That I could not have executed the operation without Noske's agreement (with Ebert in the background) and also had to protect my officers is obvious. But only a few people have understood why I was never interrogated or charged with a crime, and why the military tribunal went the way it did, Vogel was freed from prison, etc. As a man of honour, I respected the SPD of the time by keeping my mouth shut about our cooperation for fifty years. The bastards from *Spiegel* and *Stern* would have loved to find out who was behind the operation. If it becomes impossible to avoid the truth and I blow my top, I will tell the truth, which I would prefer to avoid, not least for the SPD's sake.[6]

---

6   Copy of a letter from Pabst dated 26 June 1969, BA-MA, N 620/21.

17
The Deed and Those Responsible

Following Liebknecht's confinement in Pabst's Little Salon at around 21:30 on 15 January 1919, Pabst went next door – he knew that Rosa Luxemburg would also be 'delivered' – and mused for a while. He then decided to 'dispatch' both of them,[1] unhooked the telephone and dialled the number of the man in the Reich Chancellery whom he would later describe as his most faithful supporter: Gustav Noske.

Noske, who – according to Pabst – had earlier dropped hints that Luxemburg and Liebknecht should be eliminated, initially refused to give the order and told Pabst to seek permission from General von Lüttwitz to execute the two prisoners. Pabst countered: 'I will never get it'. Noske's response: 'Then you will have to take responsibility for what must be done.'[2]

Pabst, interpreting this as carte blanche, discussed the details with his deputy Rühle von Lilienstern and his adjutant Captain von Pflugk-Harttung.

---

1   Pabst, *Memoirs*, 65 and 68, as well as his taped interview.
2   Letter from Kranzbühler to the author dated 12 January 1993.

In Pabst's aforementioned address to former cadets, he claimed to have personally spoken with Noske and received permission to kill the two of them with the nod of Noske's head. Among Pabst's fellow former cadets, the term 'Noske's blink' was also common.

To make sure nothing went wrong, the naval squadron was also to be roped in,[3] even though enough soldiers and officers were already present in the hotel for such a 'transport'. Pabst knew that 'shock troops' from among these naval officers would combine the following: a fanatical hatred of Luxemburg and Liebknecht, unconditional obedience, cold-blooded precision and absolute discretion.[4]

'The commander of the regiment, who was assigned such a division during the fighting, could be certain that every task would be fulfilled.'[5] Captain Heinz von Pflugk-Harttung was sent to see the naval officers on a 'special mission'. Entering their quarters on In den Zelten Street, he came to an agreement with his brother Horst (Kaleu), the unit commander. Horst appointed Naval Lieutenant Hermann W. Souchon, who as group leader in turn named the three others.

All of them knew what was afoot and what had to be done: they were to kill Luxemburg and Liebknecht.

Back at the Hotel Eden, Souchon, Schulze, Stiege, von Ritgen, the two Pflugk-Harttungs, Rühle von Lilienstern and Pabst conferred in the Little Hall, next to the Little Salon in which Liebknecht sat. A decision characterized

---

3   BA-MA, PH 8V/vol. 13, 194, Pabst's testimony, as well as *Wirren*, 53f and 73.

4   See document V in the appendix to this volume.

5   *Wirren*, 53f.

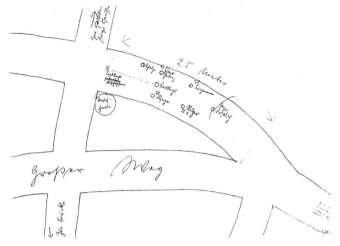

Sketches of KPD plans according to the trial records.

The Hotel Eden. Infantryman Runge, who severely injured Rosa Luxemburg with the butt of his rifle, stood in front of the revolving doors (arrow).

as a 'summary court martial' was reached.[6] Horst von Pflugk-Harttung, Stiege, Schulze, and von Ritgen were to shoot Liebknecht in the Tiergarten 'while fleeing'. This option could hardly be used for the slightly lame Rosa Luxemburg, and so Pabst opted to have her killed by an

---

6   See n. 9 and 13 <c14>.

unknown man 'from out of the crowd'.[7] That is exactly how it was described in Grabowsky's lie-filled communiqué of 16 January 1919 – which, as it happens, Souchon helped draft. All the officers volunteered to commit the deeds. The four for Liebknecht, and Souchon for Luxemburg – this fact is no longer in doubt.[8] It was chiefly Pabst's decision and that of the officers, which Noske, in Pabst's version, accepted.

Pabst commanded all of those present to keep the secret for the rest of their lives.[9] Liebknecht was then taken away, received the blows from Runge's rifle butt which Pabst had not intended, and after the car 'broke down' was shot by Pflugk-Harttung, Stiege, von Ritgen and Liepmann. Liepmann, knowing nothing of the plot, participated instinctively, as it were.[10]

In the meantime, Souchon was guarding Rosa Luxemburg in the Little Salon. Retired First Lieutenant Kurt Vogel, from the Wilmersdorf Bürgerwehr, was appointed transport leader by von Lilienstern or Pflugk-Harttung and let in on the plan.[11]

Liebknecht's escorts returned and reported their mission accomplished. Souchon went outside. Pabst allowed Luxemburg's group to depart. Runge's rifle-butt blows were, once more, unforeseen.

---

7   Personal message from Günther Nollau on 13 December 1989. On the Grabowsky communiqué, see *Dokumentation SDR*, 898ff.

8   See documents I–VII in the appendix to this volume.

9   Letter from Pflugk-Harttung to Pabst dated 3 May 1962, BA-MA, N 620/36.

10   Liepmann's testimony in the first Jorns trial as reported in the *Berliner Tageblatt*, *Vorwärts* and *Frankfurter Zeitung* on 21 April 1929.

11   See document VII in the appendix to this volume.

Rosa Luxemburg was thrown into the car like a piece of meat.

As the vehicle accelerated, von Rzewuski jumped on, struck the unconscious woman and leapt back off. We can state with almost absolute certainty that roughly forty metres later, at the corner of Kurfürstendamm and Nürnberger Straße, Souchon (who had been lying in wait) hopped onto the left footboard, leaned towards the unconscious Rosa Luxemburg, placed a Mauser pistol against her left temple and pulled the trigger.

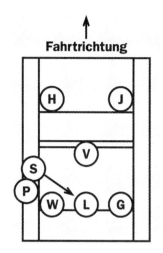

Fahrtrichtung

J: Janschkow, the driver; H: the co-driver, Hall; V: Retired First Lieutenant Vogel; S: Naval Lieutenant Souchon; L: Rosa Luxemburg; W: Infantryman Weber; G: Infantryman Grantke; P: Infantryman Poppe.

The shot did not go off at first, as he had forgotten about the gun's safety catch in the excitement. He released the catch and pulled the trigger. The shot went straight through her skull, shattering it. Rosa Luxemburg died instantly. Souchon sprang from the car and disappeared into the night.

This is also how it would be reported to Pabst afterwards.[12] Clearly, the officers' plot approved by the supreme commander fulfils the criteria for a joint murder, to which Souchon was at the very least an accomplice, as of his decision to volunteer. The great scandal is that Souchon was treated as an innocent bystander for decades, and when it

---

12   See n. 9 <c14> and document VIII, p. 202.

did emerge that he was present, he had the gall to sue in the 1970s, before judges who were out of their depth. These, in an act of positivist faith in the court records – or, if you will, in a case of political justice – not only managed to acquit an accomplice, but also absolved Jorns, Spatz (alias von Dincklage), and the 1919–20 court martial. The ruling of the superior district court against Süddeutscher Rundfunk, Bausch and Ertel is still considered valid, but really should be overturned in light of the new information that Pabst's personal files reveal.

Canaris, while not directly involved in the conspiracy, organized forged passports and broke Vogel out of prison. Later, as judge, he covered up the affair together with Jorns, who did an excellent job of obscuring the facts in tandem with Pabst. Grabowsky, meanwhile, used the WTB wire service to provide distorted or false information to an emotional bourgeois press, which lapped it up appreciatively.

And what of Noske?

This was a man whose political motto could be: 'Articles [of the law] count for nothing, the only thing that counts is success.'[13] A pre-fascist figure who, as he himself admitted, knew 'that in the Hotel Eden, where the headquarters of the division was housed, certain things were planned and done which lay outside [Pabst's] proper jurisdiction'.[14] A

---

13   Noske, defending his terroristic shoot-to-kill order in March 1919 before the National Assembly, as quoted in a highly interesting legal-historical analysis: '"Here, articles count for nothing, but rather here the only thing that counts is success…", 'Noskes Erschießungsbefehl während des Märzaufstandes in Berlin – rechtshistorisch betrachtet', *Militärgeschichtliche Mitteilungen*, edited by the Militärgeschlichtiches Forschungsamt, Freiburg, I (89), 51–79.

14   Noske, *Kiel bis Kapp*, 199.

Memorial to Rosa Luxemburg at the Landwehr Canal in Berlin.

man who deliberately and against the counsel of his advisors closed down the investigation, not wishing light to be shone on this momentous crime. A man, then, who had something to hide, yet who did not hesitate to write at the end of the Second World War: 'And I cleared away the scum and cleaned up as fast as was possible at the time',[15] who belonged to those who openly wondered 'whether anyone was going to put the troublemakers out of action'.[16]

Such a man may absolutely be capable of that which Pabst reported of him. There is no doubt about the truthfulness of Pabst's claims: Noske tacitly approved of Pabst and his officers' actions.

He was Pabst's accomplice, and Pabst was his.

---

15 Noske, *Erlebtes*, 95.
16 Noske, *Kiel bis Kapp*, 76.

On the other hand, Ebert, Scheidemann, Heine and Landsberg (who probably knew nothing of Noske's approval), proved weak in the face of the military justice system – doubtless because they, like Noske, had a soft spot for the military, whereas the names Luxemburg and Liebknecht aroused pure scorn in their hearts. Rid of their (justified) fears of a social revolution that would challenge not only war and capitalism (which did not bother the SPD leadership) but also 'Reich and nation' (with which they identified); freed of their 'Bolshevism psychosis', the former People's Deputies now believed they could return to business as usual, after re-establishing 'order' in alliance with the enemies of the republic. Yet they would not gloat for long. For what the leaders of the SPD failed to grasp, on sinking Rosa Luxemburg's body in the Landwehr Canal, was that they were sinking the Weimar Republic along with it.

Appendix
Participants in and Supporters of the Conspiracy

Wilhelm Canaris (1887–1945)

He was a cadet in 1905, Naval Lieutenant in 1909, First Naval Lieutenant in 1910 and Lieutenant Commander in 1916. By 1915, Canaris was engaged in espionage operations in Spain. In November 1918 he became a co-founder of numerous counterrevolutionary naval brigades, and Noske's adjutant shortly thereafter. In May 1919 he served as a judge in the trial before the GKSD court martial. He remained a friend and protector of the killers until his death. From 1935 to 1944 he was Hitler's most powerful intelligence chief. He also cultivated the circle of military dissidents around Hans Oster. Although he did not participate in the 20 July 1944 attempt to assassinate Hitler,

Wilhelm Canaris

he was arrested when papers were found in a safe in the Zossen army encampment, proving his earlier contacts with the resistance. He was murdered shortly before the war's end in the Flossenbürg concentration camp.

Dr Fritz Grabowsky (1886–1957)

Lieutenant in the First World War. He was a lawyer and businessman, with ties to Eduard Stadtler and Waldemar Pabst, and friendly with Canaris. Grabowsky took over as propaganda chief and director of the GKSD press office in December 1918. He delivered 'educational' lectures. Being a Jew, he always wore civilian attire at Pabst's request, to avoid 'bringing shame' upon the anti-Semitic officers working at headquarters.

Grabowsky was responsible for the 'official' mendacious communiqué issued on 16 January 1919. He had excellent contacts with the Berlin press, particularly the Wolffschen Telegrafenbüro. He co-organized the Technische Abteilung (later known as the Technische Nothilfe) in 1919, a strike-breaking unit which also spied on undesirable characters like Rudolf Breitscheid and Maximilian Harden. He was heavily involved in Pabst's Association, the Nationale Vereinigung, and participated in the Kapp Putsch.

He resurfaced in 1931–32 as the director of the *Montagsblatt*, published by Captain Ehrhardt, the former commander of the putschist naval Ehrhardt Brigade. Interned in the Oranienburg concentration camp by the Nazis in 1938, he was released by Admiral Canaris nine days later. Through Canaris, he made his way to Denmark where he engaged in foreign espionage, living in various luxury hotels seized by the Germans from 1942 to 1944. He also, presumably, worked for Canaris in intelligence-gathering operations. He went into hiding following Canaris's arrest in 1944. After the war he lived in Aachen, and renewed contact with Waldemar Pabst. When East German radio aired a drama about the night of the murder in the Hotel Eden in 1954, Grabowsky wrote to Pabst, asking: 'Do you know whether I appear in it?' Pabst responded: 'I can't say whether you do, but I would assume so, as I'm told that almost all of the "better" people from the Hotel Eden are featured, and you were most certainly among them.'

Paul Jorns (1871–1942)

Jorns served as Prussian Kriegsgerichtsrat in the armed forces' judiciary in 1900. Between 1906 and 1909 he was active in German South West Africa (now Namibia), during

Paul Jorns (far right) in 1936 at the inauguration of the People's Court. On the left sits Roland Freisler.

the colonial genocide of the Herero and Nama people. He joined the Reich Attorney General's Office in Leipzig in 1920, and was promoted to one of the attorney general's lawyers in 1925. In 1931, he represented the prosecution in the trial of German pacifist Carl von Ossietzky for treason (Ossietzky's conviction was upheld as late as 1992 by the federal court). Jorns joined the Nazi Party in 1933. In 1936 he was appointed chief state attorney in Roland Freisler's People's Court, but was forced to retire in 1937. He volunteered his services to the People's Court beginning in 1939, serving as attorney general of the Nazis' terroristic legal system and ensuring that the wheels of justice kept rolling towards a German victory.

Rudolf Liepmann (1894–19??)

Son of Privy Legal Councillor Dr Paul Liepmann. As a lieutenant in the reserve forces, he earned both classes of Iron Cross. Liepmann served in the GKSD from 1914 as an

aide-de-camp to Waldemar Pabst, with responsibility for the illegal citizens' militias. He endured anti-Semitic attacks from fellow officers. Liepmann participated in Liebknecht's transport and was one of his murderers. Before the end of his trial, he, like Vogel, was provided with a forged passport, under the name 'Lohmann'. He joined in the 1920 Kapp Putsch

A trial sketch of Rudolf Liepmann taken from the 21 April 1929 edition of the *Rote Fahne*.

in Leipzig, where he was wounded. He completed his dissertation in 1922 on 'The Policing Duties of the German Army'. His testimony was crucial to the first Jorns trial in 1929. That same year, the left-wing scholar and journalist Emil J. Gumbel met with him and reported that he was suffering from severe depression. In 1933 Liepmann was appointed as a legal clerk in the judicial service. Though he was fired in 1936 after being classified as a 'full Jew', his 'Jewish property tax' was reduced due to his 'extraordinary merits'. After managing to emigrate to Shanghai in August 1939, he disappeared from view.

Gustav Noske (1868–1946)

A journalist and a Social Democrat, he was governor of Kiel in 1918, a People's Deputy in late December 1918, commander-in-chief in the Margraviate by January 1919, and Reich minister of defence from February 1919 to March 1920. He later served as governor of Hanover. He was the only governor to remain in office after Franz von Papen's

Gustav Noske

1932 Preußenschlag or Prussia coup, as 'they remembered my work as Reich minister of defence'. Harry Graf Kessler wrote of a meeting with Noske in 1920:

Noske is manifestly a perfectly sincere and dyed-in-the-wool militarist ... He has indeed something of a bear with a nose-ring about him. Though 'unemployed', he looks prosperous enough, travels first class, wears brand new yellow boots, and consumed during the journey large quantities of ham rolls and beer. Were there not so much innocent blood on his hands, he would be a slightly comic, almost likeable figure. Where, in that immense frame of his, he keeps his social conscience and his Social Democratic red heart is another matter and his own secret.[17]

He was a major ally and promoter of Pabst, who supported all of his actions (including terroristic mass murder, as in the crushing of left-wing protests in March 1919). He adhered to Oswald Spengler's proto-fascist 'Prussian socialism'. Despite his official dismissal in 1933, Hermann Göring assured him of his personal respect and the retention of his pension. Noske expressed understanding for the Nazis and for the fact that they did not wish to work with him. Hitler described Noske in 1933 as 'an oak among these Social Democratic plants.' Noske wrote in his then-unpublished memoirs that same year, 'And I cleared away the scum and cleaned up as fast as was possible at the time'.[18] Kurt Tucholsky once wrote: 'Some murderers became governors, others died. A curse upon their memory – but one cannot curse the petite bourgeoisie.'[19]

---

17   Harry Graf Kessler, *Berlin in Lights: The Diaries of Count Harry Kessler (1918–1937)*, trans. Charles Kessler, New York: Grove Press, 2000 [1961], 129.
18   Noske, *Erlebtes*, 102.
19   *Die Weltbühne* 2, 12 January 1926, 52.

Waldemar Pabst (1881–1970)

The son of a museum director, Pabst attended various cadet
schools from 1894–99, including in
Lichterfelde. He became a career
officer in 1900. Appointed first
general staff officer of the GKSD
during the First World War, he
became the de facto commander of
this unit. Following the so-called
Christmas Skirmishes in Berlin in
1918, he transformed the GKSD
from a royal army division into

Waldemar Pabst

a heavily-armed division of the Freikorps, complete with
a propaganda department and an intelligence-gathering
unit. He was behind Noske's terroristic shoot-to-kill order
of 9 March 1919. In order to prepare the ground, he had
staged the newspaper hoax known as the 'Horrific Murders
in Lichtenberg', using the WTB with Grabowsky's help.
This gave Noske powers to execute prisoners which went
far beyond all legal states of exception and martial law
under existing German legislation. Pabst personally stiff-
ened the order for the GKSD, which he restructured into
a 40,000-man corps that same month. In June he proposed
to Noske establishing a military dictatorship, with the
Social Democrats at the head of the junta. Fearing that this
could provoke another uprising, Noske declined the suggestion, and sought to dissolve the GKSD which had since
moved its headquarters to Bendlerstraße. In riposte, Pabst
attempted to launch a coup, which was only thwarted by the

intervention of Generals von Lüttwitz and von Maercker. They did not agree with the timing.

Pabst retired from active duty. Together with his propaganda chief Grabowsky and Wolfgang Kapp, he founded a group called the Nationale Vereinigung, or national association, in preparation for a military coup; he was a major participant in the putsch launched by Kapp and Lüttwitz in 1920. Following its failure, he fled to Innsbruck under the name 'Peters'. From 1920–30 he acted as the founder and military leader of the Austrian Heimatwehr, or Home Guard, right-wing paramilitaries with the stated goal, as Pabst put it in 1924, of 'restoring a powerful state authority for the most ruthless and uncompromising struggle against Social Democracy and its stooge, Jewish democracy'.

Despite President Hindenburg's 1925 amnesty, which shielded him from prosecution for his role in the Kapp Putsch, Pabst did not return to Germany. In 1928 he denied his participation to his patron at the time, Austrian Federal Chancellor Ignaz Seipel, and claimed to still be in touch with Noske, whom he had not seen since early 1920.

Pabst, the most powerful military figure in Austria but not yet an Austrian citizen (while drawing a German officer's pension), came under renewed pressure in 1929. In November of that year he faced criminal charges in Germany for the murder of Luxemburg and Liebknecht. The proceedings were called off in March 1930. The Reichstag's blanket amnesty, passed in the same year (with the votes of the Nazis, other right-wing parties and the Communists), allowed him to return to Berlin. Expelled from Austria in June 1930, he found shelter in fascist Italy, from which he triumphantly returned to Innsbruck in November greeted by cheers of 'Heil Pabst!'.

He worked as the director of Rheinmetall Borsig AG from 1931 to 1940, running its defence and weapons division. Here, he was responsible for arms exports. In 1932 he attempted to start a White 'Fascist' International. Its foundation? Instead of 'Liberty, Equality and Fraternity – Authority, Order, and Justice.' He set up the Society for the Study of Fascism that same year, devoted to 'assessing' how much of Italian fascism could be adapted to German conditions. Members included Theodor Duesterberg, Ernst Rüdiger Starhemberg, Friedrich Wilhelm Heinz, Franz Schauweker, Eduard Stadtler, Franz Seldte, Fritz Thyssen and Hermann Göring.

Pabst only eluded the assassins who had already eliminated Kurt von Schleicher, during the so-called 'Night of the Long Knives' in 1934, by lucky accident, because he was watching the launch of an armoured battleship in Wilhelmshaven together with Canaris. He was, however, arrested. Göring released him when Canaris and Franz von Papen put in a good word. In a letter to Richard Heydrich, Pabst subsequently described himself as an 'honest and proper supporter of the National Socialist state'.

He returned to serving as an officer in the General Staff and in the war economy department under General Georg Thomas. His dismissal soon thereafter was allegedly at Hitler's personal request. In 1943, on the advice of Canaris and Thomas, Pabst did not return from a business trip in Switzerland. He enjoyed an excellent relationship with the Swiss authorities, allowing him to stay in the country long after the war's end. He did not return to West Germany until 1955, no longer fearing that the Allies would extradite him to the Soviet Union. He settled in Düsseldorf, where he later worked as the publisher of the far-right magazine *Das deutsche Wort*, voted for the far-right National Democratic Party and continued to cultivate a close relationship with the Federal Press Office. He also maintained links to the 'Amt Blank', the predecessor to the Federal Ministry of Defence under the leadership of Theodor Blank. He remained in the weapons business until his death, cutting deals with Taiwan, India and Spain. He never faced criminal prosecution in the Federal Republic.

Heinz von Pflugk-Harttung (1890–1920)

The younger brother of Horst 'Kaleu' von Pflugk-Harttung; their father was the historian and director of the Prussian Secret State Archives, Julius von Pflugk-Harttung, who in 1904 blamed Social Democracy for the spread of vegetarianism, women's dress reform and impressionist painting. He was a navigator in the First Fighter Bomber Division during the First World War and established contact with Eduard Stadtler through a 'bomber comrade'. He served as adjutant and second aide-de-camp to Waldemar Pabst in the Hotel Eden, and was one of the co-conspirators and instigator of the NSU's 'car trouble' in the Tiergarten. All records concerning criminal prosecution against his comrades-in-arms passed through his hands, after which some of them disappeared without trace.

In 1919 von Pflugk-Harttung founded the right-wing

front groups Landbund and Ferienkinder (with the illicit support of the SPD-dominated government at the time), aimed at preventing the extradition of Germans accused of war crimes in the First World War. During the Kapp Putsch he actively participated in the executions conducted in the Berlin suburb of Friedrichshagen, where he was blown up by his own hand grenades while getting into his car on 26 March 1920. His death was most likely an accident.

Horst von Pflugk-Harttung (1889–1967)

He was a cadet in 1907, a Naval Lieutenant in 1910, First Naval Lieutenant in 1913, and Lieutenant Commander in 1918. As of 1917 von Pflugk-Harttung was the commandant of a torpedo boat, and friendly with Wilhelm Canaris. After the revolution, he appointed himself to lead the naval officer 'shock troops' organized by Canaris (see chapter one). He was one of Liebknecht's murderers. With Canaris's help,

Sketch of Horst Pflugk-Harttung drawn by a court reporter, 1919.

he fled to Sweden via Denmark in 1919. There he established contact with Hermann Göring and continued to communicate with Pabst, who hoped to recruit him as a representative of the 'White International' in Sweden. He was deported to Oslo in January 1932 for his involvement in illegal arms deals on behalf of Swedish fascists. Here, he gave an interview to the newspaper *Oslo Aftenavis* in which he claimed that he received the order to kill Liebknecht from Gustav Noske. Noske publicly denied this assertion. Pflugk-Harttung then responded that the whole thing had been a misunderstanding, as Horst basically refused to speak 'about this event'.

Although supported by the commander-in-chief of the navy, Admiral Erich Raeder, Rear Admiral Magnus von Levetzow, and Vice-Admiral Adolf von Trotha, von Pflugk-Harttung was expelled from Norway. He fled to Denmark, where he worked as a spy for Canaris until he was arrested, accused of being the head of German espionage in northern Europe and expelled in 1938. Von Pflugk-Harttung worked for the German Navy's foreign intelligence service from at least 1941 onward. He was promoted to Naval Captain. By 1942 he was back in Berlin, and, rumour has it, appointed commandant of Bordeaux. He was arrested again in 1946, this time in Ireland, accused of being the 'head of the Werwölfe', Nazi partisans out to sabotage the Allied occupation. In a prisoner-of-war camp he happened to meet the future biographer of Rosa Luxemburg, John Peter Nettl, then serving as a British officer. Von Pflugk-Harttung was soon released. According to the East German Ministry for State Security, this was followed by a stint in the United States which included contacts with the CIA. He returned to West Germany in late 1949. In the 1950s he worked for the transport firm Gautz und Schmidt in Hamburg, and as a Swedish, Danish and Norwegian translator. He re-established contact with Pabst in 1962 and maintained it until his death. He never faced prosecution in the Federal Republic.

Ulrich von Ritgen (1894–1969)

Son of Hugo von Ritgen, planning director for the city of Wetzlar. He became a cadet in 1913, a Naval Lieutenant in 1915, and a First Naval Lieutenant in 1917. He was a member of the Pflugk-Harttung naval squadron and one of Karl Liebknecht's murderers. In the 1920s he was active in the so-called Defence of the Ruhr Region as a counterfeiter of French bank-notes. His house was searched by

Ulrich von Ritgen, 1926–1927

the American Counterintelligence Corps in 1946 following an accusation by his father-in-law (of involvement in the 1922 murder of the foreign minister, Walther Rathenau). Instead, evidence of his part in the murder of Liebknecht was found, forcing the German police to arrest him on American orders. In prison, he was treated as a 'hero of freedom'. Von Ritgen was rapidly acquitted by the Kassel superior district court. Afterwards he continued to fear (not entirely without justification) arrest by the authorities in the Eastern occupied zone. He commented on Ertel's docu-drama several months before his death in 1969, stating that 'the author has for the most part depicted it correctly'.

Hans Rühle von Lilienstern (1884–1966)

On 15 January 1919 he was a captain, first orderly officer to Wilhelm Pabst and a co-conspirator. Under the Third

Reich he progressed to the rank of lieutenant general. After the war, he lived as a businessman in Karlsruhe and continued to have contact with Pabst. No further information about him is known.

Otto Wilhelm Runge (1875–1945)

A welder by training, he struck Liebknecht and Luxemburg with the butt of his rifle after being bribed to do so by Captain Petri, though he failed to kill either of them. In 1919 he first went into hiding in Liepmann's apartment, then, at Pabst's urging, crossed the Danish border under the name 'Dünnwald'. He received

Sketch of Otto Runge drawn by a court reporter, 1919.

repeated support in the form of bribe money. Runge was the only participant to serve a prison sentence, from 1919 to 1921. He wrote countless letters from prison confessing to his crime, some of which came close to the truth ('The orders came from Captain Pabst'), but were ignored by the military tribunal. The decision against reopening the case, for example, read as follows: 'The applicant [Runge] bases his case on the new assertion that he carried out the criminal acts on orders from his superiors. This assertion is negligible insofar as, even if he did receive such orders, they were not legitimate commands bearing on matters of duty which he was obliged to follow, but rather orders to commit crimes or offences (Article 47 of the Military

Criminal Code). There is no evidence to suggest that the applicant did not realize this.' A clever line of argument, which German courts unfortunately did not apply to Nazi criminals after the Second World War.

Following his release, Runge lived under the name 'Radolf' in Berlin. He was nevertheless recognized and attacked twice, by workers from the Siemens complex in 1925 and by a group of unemployed workers in 1931. He received financial support from the Nazi state in 1933. Runge wrote many letters pleading with, among others, Pabst and Wilhelm II in Holland. Aged seventy, he was arrested by Communists in May 1945. After questioning, he was transferred by the chief prosecutor of Greater Berlin, Max Berger, to the Soviet Commandant's office in Prenzlauer Allee 173 – against the protests of those who captured him, who would have preferred to mount a show trial. Here he died in unknown circumstances after a final interrogation by the NKVD.[20]

Bruno Schulze (1895–19??)

Naval cadet in 1914, naval lieutenant in 1916. Member of the Pflugk-Harttung naval squadron. Schulze was present in the transport and murder of Liebknecht, but did not fire his weapon. No further information about him is known.

---

20   See Doris Kachulle, *Waldemar Pabst und die Gegenrevolution*, Berlin: Organon, 2007, 109ff.

Hermann W. Souchon (1894–1982)

Nephew of Admiral Wilhelm Souchon, the governor of Kiel who was designated to negotiate with the mutinous sailors in November 1918, before being replaced by Gustav Noske. He became a naval lieutenant in 1915 and was a member of the Pflugk-Harttung naval squadron. Souchon was not involved in Liebknecht's transport and appeared as a 'crown witness' before the GKSD court

Hermann Wilhelm Souchon in 1969

martial, testifying to the officers' 'innocence' and providing a sworn affidavit. In May 1919 he was stationed in Zossen with the Assault Battalion Schmidt. In 1920 he fled to Finland, where he worked as a bank clerk. In 1932 he sought renewed contact with Waldemar Pabst, envisioning himself as a representative of the latter's 'White International' in Finland. Souchon returned to Germany in 1935, and rose through the ranks during the Second World War to become a colonel in the air force. He turned up again as the plaintiff in the 1969–71 trial of *Souchon v. Süddeutscher Rundfunk, Bausch and Ertel* before several Stuttgart courts. He won by lying once again, as is proven in this volume.

Kriegsgerichtsrat Spatz (1896–1974)

The man identified in the sources as 'Spatz' was almost certainly Hans Günther von Dincklage, a member of the

GKSD and Jorns's successor in investigating the case. He prevented Vogel's extradition and covered up the double homicide even more skilfully than Jorns. He worked for Joseph Goebbels's propaganda ministry in the 1930s and later established a spy ring in France while serving in Wilhelm Canaris's espionage department. He enjoyed a romantic relationship from 1940 to 1950 with the French fashion designer, Coco Chanel, who, under the alias 'Westminster', also conducted operations for Nazi Germany. Dincklage fled to Switzerland in 1944. Chanel followed him after the liberation of Paris without being stopped by authorities.[21]

Heinrich Stiege (1895–1968)

Son of Rear Admiral Oskar Stiege. A cadet in 1913, naval lieutenant in 1915. Member of the Pflugk-Harttung naval squadron and one of Karl Liebknecht's murderers. In 1920 he was active in Hamburg as a businessman, and in 1929 became a manager of the Deutsche Gesellschaft zur Schädlingsbekämpfung, or 'Degesch', a pest control company which later became the sole manufacturer of Zyklon B.

In 1932 he was an authorized agent for Degesch, and by 1936 had risen to department director of *Deutsche Gold- und Silberscheideanstalt* ('Degussa'), of which Degesch was a subsidiary. Both companies belonged to the IG Farben corporation. Because Stiege's grandmother was Jewish, he was labelled a 'second-class crossbreed' and prevented

---

21 See Hal Vaughan, *Sleeping with the Enemy: Coco Chanel, Nazi Agent*, London: Chatto & Windus, 2011.

from joining the company's board of directors. In order to revive his naval career despite having a 'non-Aryan' grandmother, he wrote a letter to Admiral Erich Raeder in which he attested to having been present in the Tiergarten on 15 January 1919. Following the outbreak of war, he became a lieutenant commander in 1939 and a corvette captain in 1944. Classified as 'not implicated' in the crimes of Nazi Germany in 1945, he sought to return to his job at Degussa the next year. However, his letter to Raeder fell into the hands of a works council. In response, Stiege initiated a de-Nazification trial against himself for his participation in Liebknecht's execution.

The case was dismissed, as no new evidence was produced despite intensive efforts, and the judgement from 1919 (thanks to Noske) was upheld.

Stiege returned to Degussa in Frankfurt in the 1950s. In 1967, when he had retired to Allgäu, he was visited by Dieter Ertel. Ertel read a transcript from the GKSD military tribunal aloud to the aimable old man. 'Judge: Where did you aim? Stiege: At the body, perhaps the lower back, if one can say that.' Stiege turned green and began gasping for air, before confirming the officers' plans to Ertel.

Kurt Vogel (1889–1963)

Having served as a pilot officer, Vogel was already a retired first lieutenant by 15 January 1919. He acted as a liaison between the Hotel Eden and the Wilmersdorf Bürgerwehr. Formally, he did not belong to Pabst's staff. He was retroactively pushed into the latter in a 'document' designed to rescue him from the state prosecutor and place him under the jurisdiction of the military courts. Leo Jogiches accused him of Rosa Luxemburg's murder in a 13 February 1919 article in the *Rote Fahne*. In the trial, he was only convicted of 'dereliction of duty and disposing of a corpse'. Three days after the verdict was announced, he fled to Holland

Sketch of Kurt Vogel drawn by a court reporter, 1919.

with the help of the division staff. Here, he was imprisoned.

Vogel was granted amnesty by the Berlin district court on 23 December 1920, citing the 4 August 1920 amnesty which forgave all crimes committed with the aim of defeating a 'highly treasonous enterprise against the Reich'. However, the amnesty law excluded crimes that threatened life. The district court thus assumed that Rosa Luxemburg was engaged in a highly treasonous enterprise against the Reich, and that Vogel had not killed her out of 'defence'. Following intense public uproar, state prosecutor Ortmann filed an objection.

Shortly thereafter, the amnesty was withdrawn by the superior district court. Vogel's participation was disregarded, however, and the court clung to the assertion the 'January Movement of the year 1919 could not be seen as highly treasonous'. Vogel was permitted to leave his detention camp around the same time. His second bid for amnesty failed in 1925, but the verdict against Vogel was definitively repealed in 1928.

Vogel blackmailed his officer comrades, particularly Pabst, from exile. In 1933 he was 'brought home' to Nazi Germany on the express wishes of the Reich Minister of Labour. Back in Berlin, Vogel often boasted of his participation in the murders of Luxemburg and (!) Liebknecht. Here, he happened to meet the future director of the Institute of Contemporary History in Munich (1959–72), Helmut Krausnick.

Vogel left Berlin on 6 February 1949 and 'moved to an unknown address, without giving notice of his departure'.

Documents

Document I:[1] Memory Log of a Conversation with Waldemar Pabst

Participants: Waldemar Pabst, Frau Pabst, an editor of the magazine *Das deutsche Wort*, Dr Erger (historian at the Aachen College of Pedagogy), Dr Gustav Strübel, Süddeutscher Rundfunk, Dieter Ertel.

The conversation took place on Friday, 28 January 1966, from 16:00 to 19:00 at the apartment of the married couple Pabst in Düsseldorf, Windscheidstraße 19. The editor of the magazine *Das deutsche Wort* and Herr Dr Erger scarcely intervened in the conversation and were evidently only invited by Pabst to serve as witnesses.

Herr Pabst began with a long monologue about the 'internal leadership', which already existed during his time albeit not under such a lofty title. He then told of an

---

1 Copies of documents I–V provided with the kind permission of Dieter Ertel.

encounter he had had in the express train from Switzerland to Germany, not long after his interview with *Der Spiegel*.

A gentleman in the same compartment looked him over, noticed his – Pabst's – luggage tag, inquired about his identity, introduced himself with the name 'Liebknecht' and asked if they might speak. He had seen Pabst's picture in *Spiegel*. The two gentlemen then conversed for some time in the aisle of the express train. Liebknecht, a nephew of Karl Liebknecht who was murdered on Pabst's orders, finally stated:

'From your standpoint, I can understand your course of action in 1919.' He went on to ask why Pabst had not killed Noske back then, and worked together with the Communists. Had he done so, the National Socialists would never have ruled in Germany. Pabst: his interlocutor in the express train was not himself a Communist.

Pabst cited several justifications for the murders of Liebknecht and Luxemburg which he had already advanced elsewhere: he could not have handed Rosa Luxemburg and Karl Liebknecht over to a proper judiciary, as none existed in early 1919. Liebknecht and Luxemburg were being searched for with Wanted posters. The Bolshevist go-between for the Spartacus League, Karl Radek, had already been arrested several weeks before.[2] Radek, however, was released by the Communist [!] police chief Eichhorn, and he, Pabst, had not wanted to run the same risk again. (Herr Pabst obviously forgot here that Eichhorn was no longer in

---

2   Not quite accurate, and pushed forward by Pabst. Karl Radek would only be arrested in February 1919 (see n. 14 <c12>). That said, the Reinhard Brigade that arrested Radek was under the command of the GKSD.

office by early 1919. When this was pointed out to him, he mentioned the fear of not controlling, or losing control of, the Moabit prison. Pabst repeatedly said something to the effect of 'Had they caught me, they would have killed me.' Times of civil war have their own laws.)

Pabst had not asked his division commander, General von Hofmann, for permission to commit the murders, as he was sure that Hofmann – a 'terminally ill' man, according to Pabst – would have hesitated. Pabst did not inform his division commander about the killing of Liebknecht and Luxemburg until 16 January, at 4:30 in the morning, by telephone.[3] Hofmann thanked Pabst for not placing the responsibility to decide on him and added: 'You will have to carry this and be reminded of it for your entire life.' The lieutenant general then assumed responsibility for what had occurred.

Over the course of the conversation, Pabst went on to state: he neither instigated nor approved of the rifle-butt blows from the hussar Runge: he had even summoned Runge and 'told him off'. Runge had been bribed by a railroad officer from his staff, which numbered roughly eighty men. The officer had not been privy to the other murder plans.

Pabst claimed not to know whether Runge had also been encouraged to shoot Wilhelm Pieck (as both later consistently claimed). It would have been – according to Pabst – well-nigh impossible to perform such an execution in a hotel lobby. Under no circumstances would he have

---

3   Pabst later corrected his statement, claiming that he informed von Hofmann in person at 03:00 hours.

had Pieck killed of his own accord, even if Pieck had not betrayed his comrades. Furthermore, Pieck was 'not valuable enough' to him. Pabst, whose memory, by the way, functions excellently for an eighty-five-year-old, claimed not to remember whether the arrest and execution of Luxemburg's friend Leo Jogiches was a result of Wilhelm Pieck's betrayal.

Had the revolution not occurred, he, Pabst, would have been in line for a promotion to major on 18 November 1918. The naval officers who accompanied and shot Karl Liebknecht were, as members of the Ehrhardt Brigade, subordinate to the Garde-Kavallerie-Schützen-Division.

Asked for a characterization of his prisoners, Pabst said: 'Liebknecht was a coward.' As 'proof' he cited the fact that the Communist leader had denied being Liebknecht. A naval officer – not Pflugk-Harttung – tore open his coat and identified him by the monogram on his shirt. Rosa Luxemburg by contrast sat calmly in a corner of Pabst's room – Pabst sat in the other, at his desk – and read *Faust*, although she, as Pabst put it, must have known that nothing good awaited her. (During the waiting period, the soldiers who were to play the 'crowd' were assembled.)

On cutting off Kriegsgerichtsrat Kurtzig and entrusting Jorns with the entire investigation: Kurtzig had been a 'jobsworth'. Jorns had the task of preventing a trial by 'correcting' the witnesses' testimony, and made an honest effort to do so. Pabst: 'Jorns accomplished his difficult task splendidly.' Pabst confirmed that he was effectively Jorns's judge. He was even present at the witness interrogations. Before the deed and immediately afterwards, no one had ever thought about a trial. Only following the 'mishaps', the public uproar and the government's 'capitulation' were they forced to act out the farce. The government had known perfectly well that it was a farce, but wanted to play along [...].

In Pabst's view it is obvious that the proceedings could have been struck down had the SPD government been more committed to 'their' Garde-Kavallerie-Schützen-Division and its actions. (He forgets that the SPD was anything but a monolithic bloc at that time. Particularly after the murders, and the battle for the Marstall Stables, many defected to the Communists.) In Pabst's opinion, he saved democracy with this liquidation, and Noske had afterward 'extended his hand' to him for it.

Pabst on Noske: 'A fine chap.' Noske was merely forced to take his comrades, who repeatedly sought to sway their 'Gustav', into too much consideration. Pabst recalls an exchange with Noske in which he told him: 'Herr Noske, we both know it: you're trying to cheat me, and I'm trying to cheat you.' Upon being asked, Pabst admitted without hesitation that he himself was the most powerful man in Berlin in January 1919. Together with all military and para-military units, the Bürgerwehr which he had personally organized was also under his command.

Pabst on Lieutenant Marloh, who organized a massacre of members of the People's Navy Division in 1919 and was exonerated by a military tribunal: 'A pig.' However, Marloh was then dishonourably discharged from the brigade.

Pabst described his officers who became famous through the Liebknecht-Luxemburg case, all of whom volunteered to conduct the operation, as follows: the Pflugk-Harttung brothers were 'fanatical soldiers'. (Capt. [Heinz] Pfl.-H. was an orderly officer – 'O2' – under Pabst.) Lieutenant Liepmann was a very decent man, who 'lost his nerve a bit' later on. He belonged to the division's press department led by First Lieutenant Grabowski. Grabowski – like Liepmann, a Jew – had been an extraordinarily capable man. He came from a highly respected and nationalist-minded Berlin family.

Kriegsgerichtsrat Ehrhardt, who led the main trial, had been a 'proper and somewhat overly soft man'. He was used as a figurehead, while Canaris pulled the strings in the trial as an observer, with Pabst's and Jorns's agreement. Pabst admits that the trial was a sorry affair, somehow beneath his '*niveau*'; but he had no other option left. The division felt abandoned by the SPD government's capitulation. This had also been a reason for his participation in the Kapp Putsch.

Luxemburg's murderer, First Lieutenant Vogel, completely lost his nerve later on. After his sentencing he broke down and screamed: 'I have to get out of here!' He was afraid the Communists would storm the prison and kill him. The officer who got Vogel out was Canaris. (Herr Pabst requests that this information not be used.)

Pabst on Vogel: 'He would cost us a lot of money later on'. Following his escape to Holland, Vogel blackmailed his former comrades in the Garde-Kavallerie-Schützen-Division.

Pabst's order stated that First Naval Lieutenant Souchon should shoot Rosa Luxemburg. Souchon was to wait for

Luxemburg's transport with other soldiers at a certain point along the route and carry out the deed. It should then be presented as if an unknown person had fired from out of an angry mob. (Herr Pabst also asks us not to use this testimony.)

In truth, the 'mob' at that time was only the soldiers; there was no one on the street without some type of uniform. Lieutenant Vogel lost his nerve after the mishap with Runge and fired the fatal shot without having an order to do so.[4] A further 'mishap' had been to throw Rosa Luxemburg into the Landwehr Canal. The decision to kill Liebknecht and Rosa Luxemburg was 'not a spontaneous decision'. It is interesting how Pabst reached the decision to also kill Rosa Luxemburg.

A regiment commander, a nobleman and a Catholic, came to the division headquarters one day (implying that Pabst intercepted him before he made it to the general) and asked for permission to allow Rosa Luxemburg to address the troops. The officer had heard a speech by Rosa Luxemburg, was enthused by her and – according to Pabst – 'regarded her to be a saint', 'a new Messiah' with tremendous sense of purpose. Pabst today: 'At that moment I completely understood how dangerous Frau Luxemburg was. She was more dangerous than all the others, even those bearing arms.' The regiment commander in question was immediately relieved from his duties, on Pabst's orders.

Incidentally, Pabst recalled his satisfaction on 24 December 1918 when he was able to conclude: 'The troops

---

4   Ertel later explained they had been so convinced of Vogel's guilt that they didn't even notice that Pabst made no comment on the matter.

are shooting!' Until that point it was not entirely clear whether the division would continue to obey their old officers, although Pabst had personally worked on all of them, down to the last non-commissioned officer. He confirmed that the officers held in pre-trial detention were provided with machine guns and flamethrowers. More precisely: the prison commander, Frigate Captain v.[on] Zitzewitz, requested the weapons and distributed them to the prisoners in case of an attack on the Moabit prison.

The former hussar Otto Runge was, according to Pabst, a member of the Berlin magistracy for a while after 1933.

Herr Pabst expresses his willingness to do a television interview, on condition that the questions be submitted to him in writing beforehand.

2 February 1966

For accuracy:[5]
   (Dr Gustav Strübel)
   (Dieter Ertel)

---

5   The original copy features the handwritten signatures of both Strübel and Ertel.

Document II: Memory Log of a Second Conversation with Retired Major Waldemar Pabst[6]

Participants: Waldemar Pabst, Dr Gustav Strübel, Dieter Ertel. Frau Dr Hoffmann, who also wrote down several parts of the conversation, was present as a witness. The discussion took place on Tuesday, 3 May 1966 in the sanatorium of Dr Büdingen in Konstanz.

After debating several preconditions for the television interview[7] we have planned with him, Herr Pabst described a meeting with the USPD People's Deputy Emil Barth at the Wildpark train station near Potsdam, where the GKSD disembarked.

The first transport train which carried the division staff arrived at the station in the early morning greeted by trumpets. Here, multiple revolutionary delegations and councils led by Emil Barth greeted the soldiers. Barth called to the division commander, Lieutenant General von Hofmann: 'Hey, you, come over here!' Pabst asked v. Hofmann to speak with Barth, as he knew the Berliner dialect, and called back: 'Hey, you, come over here!' The following dialogue then took place, according to Pabst's account:

BARTH: I am your superior!

PABST: Have you lost your mind?

BARTH: I am People's Deputy Barth.

PABST: People's Deputy? Who appointed you? Were you elected by the people?

---

6   The original copy of the minutes is signed by Dr Gustav Strübel and Dieter Ertel.

7   The interview never took place.

BARTH: (no answer)

PABST: Where were you in the war?

BARTH: In the munitions factories in Spandau.

Hearing this, Pabst claims, he excoriated Barth for the munitions workers' strike in early 1918, which was largely carried by workers from Spandau. Barth demanded that the GKSD host speakers who would educate the troops politically. Pabst: 'We don't need that, we already did it ourselves.' Barth introduced his companions, the last one being the 'Councillor of the Deserters'. Pabst, who had equipped his soldiers with a kind of police baton, responded: 'Clear the train platform in three minutes, or expect a thrashing!'[8]

The GKSD set up their division quarters in Nikolassee, erected roadblocks and took precautions to ensure that no uninvited guests could enter. Barth attempted to prevent the planned march through the Brandenburg Gate, but failed. Neither did his pleas to march without weapons or at least without ammunition get through to Pabst. At the time of its arrival on 10 December, the GKSD consisted of roughly 16,000 men.

Prior to the 15 January 1919 deployment which practically ended the first Spartacus uprising, Pabst did not know exactly where Karl Liebknecht and Rosa Luxemburg were staying. He had only received indications that the pair were in the western half of Berlin. Pabst had just begun establishing his own 'espionage' department. Contacts existed to the 'Reichsbürgerrat', in which a banker named Marx played a role.

8   On this, see a description of the incident from Barth's perspective: Emil Barth, *Aus der Werkstatt der deutschen Revolution*, Berlin: Hoffman, 1919, 75.

Pabst came to the Garde-Kavallerie-Schützen Division in March 1918 on Ludendorff's orders, instructed to mould it into a riflemen (infantry) division, which by his own account worked out excellently. The division had been a renowned elite infantry unit on the Western Front. Pabst was discharged in December 1919. An official newsletter recorded that he had 'retired from active duty for the granting of his pension'.

Pabst denies having any prior knowledge that infantryman Runge struck Liebknecht with the butt of his rifle. He even claims to have learned of it for the first time through us.

Pabst reported the end of Karl Liebknecht and Rosa Luxemburg to then-Major von Schleicher, who was staying with General Commander Lüttwitz, on the very night of the murders via telephone. Schleicher: 'Pabst, you have done a fine job!' Pabst rejected the implication of these congratulations. He was merely passing on 'official information from the transport leader'. Early the next day, Schleicher, who had travelled back to Groener in Kassel (he was Groener's intermediary with Lüttwitz), called for arrests to be made: 'Sacrifices must be offered to the popular mood.' Otherwise, Ebert threatened to resign. Pabst: 'Then let him resign!'

Schleicher gave Pabst the 'comradely advice to allow himself to be suspended and initiate proceedings against himself', which Pabst comments on by saying: 'I got to know Herr Schleicher very well that night.' Pabst received orders from Schleicher to attend a meeting with the five People's Deputies and Lüttwitz, in order to decide on the next steps in the Liebknecht/Luxemburg case. He says that his troops were already poised to arrest the government should it order the arrest of him and his officers.

As we know, Pabst attempted to establish a dictatorship in the years 1919 and 1920, although 'Noske would have been preferable' to him, having greater support among the people as an SPD man. He had several meetings with Noske about this question. Pabst himself says that he 'did not yet see through all of the (political) matters' in December 1918.

He would only tell the examining magistrate Jorns about the true facts of the murder of Liebknecht and Rosa Luxemburg some time later. A correction: he did not call division commander Lieutenant General v. Hofmann in the early morning around 05:00, but rather woke him up personally. Upon further questioning, Pabst admitted that the officer who bribed infantryman Runge was Captain Petri.

The row with the noble regiment commander about Rosa Luxemburg, mentioned in the first conversation, took place in Dahlem. Rosa Luxemburg had endorsed the calls for revolution in January 1919 and was thus to him, Pabst, equally guilty of the bloodshed.

Pabst states that Kriegsgerichtsrat Jorns was appointed by the government. Following the observation that the SPD at the time had by no means been 'without a Fatherland', but was rather docile as a lamb, Pabst responds: 'It drank the poison we gave it.'

Stuttgart, 5 May 1966

For accuracy:

(Dr Gustav Strübel)

(Dieter Ertel)

Document III: Memory Log of a Third Conversation with Retired Major Waldemar Pabst[9]

Participants: Waldemar Pabst, Frau Pabst, Hans Beuthner (Süddeutscher Rundfunk), Dieter Ertel (Süddeutscher Rundfunk). The conversation took place on Wednesday, 7 December 1966, from 17:00 to 19:15 in the apartment of Herr Pabst, Düsseldorf, Windscheidstr. 19.

The most important part of the conversation for us was that which revolved around the identity of the man who shot and killed Rosa Luxemburg from the footboard of the transport vehicle on 15 January 1919. This part went as follows:

I informed Pabst that during our study of records and sources, we had come into possession of material which cast Naval Lieutenant Hermann Wilhelm Souchon in a very suspicious light. We had concluded, among other things, that Souchon (who received the order from Pabst to shoot Frau Luxemburg) had in fact ridden in the automobile.

Pabst said the following in response: 'No, he did not ride with them. Souchon jumped onto the footboard and shot Rosa Luxemburg from there.' This statement aligned with Pabst's plan, according to which the assassination of Frau Luxemburg would be portrayed as a shot fired from the midst of an angry mob.

In response I asked Herr Pabst why, given this state of affairs, the division staff had allowed the taint of having

---

9 The original copy of the minutes is signed by Hans Beuthner and Dieter Ertel.

murdered Rosa Luxemburg to stick to First Lieutenant Vogel. Was it because proceedings against Vogel as the leader of the transport would have to be initiated anyway, and additional officers were not to be dragged into it? Herr Pabst confirmed this interpretation and added that Herr Souchon had been a remarkably popular and capable officer. In this context Herr Pabst also informed us that First Lieutenant Vogel was aware of the murder plan. He drove Frau Luxemburg into infantryman Runge's path on his own initiative, assuming that Runge would relieve the officers of this dirty business. According to his (Pabst's) plan, Frau Luxemburg should of course have boarded the automobile by herself, as a healthy person. Looking back at Runge's actions towards Liebknecht and Rosa Luxemburg, Pabst remarked verbatim: 'That was terrible luck, that precisely this lad was on sentry duty down there.' He felt that Runge ruined his whole plan. He added that Vogel's orders were to bring the deceased Rosa Luxemburg to the morgue; Souchon, by contrast, was to jump off immediately after the gunshot and disappear into the dark of night (as did in fact occur).

With regard to Captain Petri, who bribed Runge, Pabst recalled that he chided him and dismissed him from his staff. He barely knew Petri before 15 January, as he was a new arrival to the staff. Pabst was in urgent need of a railway advisor at the time and assigned this task to Petri.

Pabst went on to tell the following episode from the later life of First Lieutenant Vogel, who until now had been regarded as the shooter and disappeared to Holland following the deed, where he continued to blackmail his former

comrades-in-arms: Vogel returned from Holland after the
Nazi takeover in 1933 and called on Herr Pabst in elegant,
almost dandyish attire right after he became the director
of Rheinmetall-Borsig in Berlin. Pabst feared that Vogel
would try to get money from him again. Instead Vogel
proudly announced that he had been offered the position
of an assistant director in Goebbels's propaganda ministry. Vogel subsequently took up this post, but was sacked
within days because – Pabst presumes – Goebbels's people
had found out that Vogel financed his life in Holland almost
entirely through freeloading and blackmail.

Herr Pabst answered in the negative to the question of
whether he had known prior to the arrival of Liebknecht
and Rosa Luxemburg that these two would be delivered to
his door, so to speak. He first learned of their arrest when
the pair arrived. We then wanted to know if the shooters,
who according to Pabst had volunteered, knew what it
was about. (The naval officers were not in the Hotel Eden
when they volunteered, but rather in the staff quarters of
their squadron in In den Zelten.) Pabst replied that they
had known. He had informed a captain from his staff, Herr
Rühle von Lilienstern, and directed him to constitute the
squads out of volunteers.

Pabst also said of the immediate consequences of the liquidation: on 16 January, at 06:00 in the morning, a Herr
Rauscher (allegedly the government's press officer) called
him to say that 'noble blood had been spilled' that night,
and the people's wrath would demand sacrifices. To the
question of how the preliminary investigation by a military court came about, Pabst said: at the meeting that took

place on 16 January in the Reich Chancellery between the five People's Deputies, Generals von Lüttwitz and von Hofmann and Pabst himself, Landsberg and Scheidemann[10] demanded immediate arrests in light of the popular mood. Ebert and Noske had been significantly more moderate. Lüttwitz ultimately offered a court-martial investigation. Ebert took up this suggestion and managed to get the two gentlemen to agree to it.

Towards the end of the conversation Pabst considered the situation at that time of the Garde-Kavallerie-Schützen-Division, which had just moved to accepting volunteers. They had bad luck with some of these volunteers, as many people (including the unemployed) 'came from the other side'. But they had no way of preventing the entry of unwanted elements completely.

Pabst said of Ebert: 'We couldn't have had a better man back then.' Ebert was much cleverer and more capable than Hindenburg.

On the USPD leader Ledebour: he was one of the worst fanatics, talked a terrible amount and spat in such a way while doing so that Pabst always tried to step away from him. To our question of whether Pabst would also have killed Ledebour if he had fallen into his hands, rather than those of the soldiers under the commandant's office, Pabst said no. Ledebour had not been that important, after all.

According to Pabst, the leader of Liebknecht's transport, then-Lieutenant Commander Horst von Pflugk-Harttung,

---

10   Scheidemann could not have been present on 16 January 1919, as he only returned from Kassel on 17 January. See Philipp Scheidemann, *Memoiren eines Sozialdemokraten*, vol. 2, Dresden: Reissner, 1928, 347ff.

is still alive and lives in Hamburg. Pabst's closest collaborator in the Luxemburg/Liebknecht case and in the Kapp Putsch, Dr Fritz Grabowski (Pabst's first lieutenant and press officer at the time of the Liebknecht/Luxemburg murders) lived in Aachen until recently and died three years ago.

Pabst filled out his earlier account of his experience in the express train, recalling that Liebknecht's nephew who approached him in the train, D. Eng. Liebknecht, said to him: 'If my uncle had caught you back then, he would have killed you too.' Pabst answered in the affirmative to our question if he had still been a staunch monarchist at that time, and added: 'I still am today.'

Apart from that, Frau Pabst mentioned to us that the deputy chief of police, a government director by the name of Körner, owned an extraordinarily comprehensive special collection of documents and photos from the time of the revolution. He can be reached at: Aachen, Diepenhenden 32, Tel. Aachen 23 5 53, work phone 40 61.

Stuttgart, 9 December 1966

(Hans Beuthner)
(Dieter Ertel)

Document IV: Letter from Waldemar Pabst to Dieter Ertel, 18 May 1967[11]

W. Pabst
Düsseldorf, 18.5.1967.
Windscheidstraße 19
Telephone 62 79 25

Dear Herr Ertel!

The German television news service announced on 6.5.67 that you managed, fifty years after the execution of Frau Luxemburg, to discover the man who really fired the deadly shot. Compliments to your serendipity and my obfuscation tactics at the time!

I have of course received from various sides these statements made by your news service, which many papers repeated, some condensed, and some in full.

I would have appreciated it if you had informed me of this intention before publication and sent me the planned text for my perusal. I am convinced I would have found a significantly better formulation. I certainly understand that you might wish, indeed, must wish, that you have the 'right of primogeniture' to more clearly elucidate your discovery than did *Spiegel* on 13.2.67, and by the same token I must request your understanding that our agreed cooperation will not be disturbed by accidental news reports and that – as occurred – 'murder' will not be spoken of – this goes

---

11 Typewritten on printed letterhead with name, address and telephone number, signed by hand; letterspaced words in the original are rendered in italics.

for me and my subordinates at the time. It would appear that your news service lacks a true legal expert who would know what the listed preconditions are for a 'murder' in the German criminal code.

For me, the question arises: 'How can I protect my former subordinate Souchon whose name *Spiegel* has, quite unnecessarily, dragged into the public eye?'

Herr S.[ouchon] did no more back then than volunteer to carry out orders issued by me, and not out of a desire to murder, but rather out of the same motivations that guided me as well, namely: ending the mutual killing of Germans in the interests of Moscow and eliminating the two most guilty for this bloodshed, Liebknecht–Luxemburg. Had these Spartacists got their hands on me under the domestic political conditions of the time they would have eliminated me, just as the frenzied Communist masses did with so many of my comrades-in-arms.

You know very well that I carried out my solution for Germany, *not* for me – and with great reluctance – but it was inevitable, or else our homeland would have become a satellite state of Moscow, the goal which both of these Communist leaders intended and whose frustration I saw as my duty. The bravery of our unit and the impeccable cooperation with such German-minded men as Ebert and Noske made the success of my task possible. Both were smart enough to accept the facts I established on the ground, which of course were also chiefly beneficial to their party. And that is why they were also quite reluctant to involve me in any prosecution.

In closing I note:

1.) Better cooperation between us appears absolutely necessary to me.

2.) Your news service should kindly cease conflating a 'politically necessary action' in Germany's interest at the time with 'murder'.

I would be grateful, my dear Herr Ertel, if you would make the effort to convey the same in this spirit, however *without publishing this letter*, so that the wretched topic has settled down by the time your television show is broadcast, which – as promised – will also convey the context and motivations of my actions.

Yours sincerely
(W. Pabst)

Document V: Letter from Waldemar Pabst to Dieter Ertel, 30 May 1967[12]

W. Pabst
Düsseldorf, 30.5.1967.
Windscheidstraße 19
Telephone 62 79 25

Dear Herr Ertel!

Many thanks for your comprehensive letter dated 26.5. –

I would like to comment on almost every sentence. I did not even mention in my letter dated 18.5. that not primarily the question of priority, but rather of initial propaganda was the cause that allowed your news service to appear, for that is obvious, that's what this institution is made for. The original text of this press announcement interests me all the more; could you send it to me? So far I am only familiar with the AP report.

I cannot agree with the skilful formulation whereby you conflate 'murderer' with 'executioner'. For to be an executioner is a *profession* in all civilized states, at least it is viewed as such by the majority. Making this term even less fitting for a man like Souchon, given that he volunteered to carry out my instruction, not as a paid, professional task, but as something that could bring him nothing but trouble and inconvenience. Therefore if you want to classify Souchon within a particular group of people, there is only one word

---

12   Typewritten on printed letterhead with name, address and telephone number, signed by hand; letterspaced words in the original are rendered in cursive.

for it: he was a fanatic, but then so was I and my people, not only S.[ouchon] but, for example, v. Pflug[k]-Hart[t] ung etc., Noske too (see my order to shoot and the way he defended it), and on the opposing side – Liebknecht and Luxemburg. Albeit with the not insignificant difference that these two fanatics would have first unleashed their fanaticism to overthrow the German social order via a bloody revolution. And therein lies the decisive point – we did not return home as fanatics, we did not contemplate bloodshed, we'd had more than enough of it after over 4 years of war. We only became fanatics when we returned to Berlin and saw what Spartacist fanaticism had caused. Please do not omit to clearly highlight and emphasize and underline that it was Ebert and his party who would never, ever, have been able to deal with the Spartacist revolution without our help, which they requested. – And without their own fanatic, Noske.

And with that I arrive at your question! Of course Noske, Ebert and Wissel[l] knew what game was being played. Would they otherwise have shaken my hand when I was forced to go to the Reich Chancellery in the small hours of 15.1.19,[13] summoned by the Supreme Army Command, in order to report on the events of the previous night to the five People's Deputies, and reassured me again with clasped hands, while absolute understanding (if not more!) lay in Noske's expression? Landsberg and to some extent Scheidemann did – as I am aware – attempt to initiate proceedings against me, but I rather doubt whether this was in earnest. It was more out of fear that the street would have their precious skins in the end!

---

13   He meant, of course, 16.1.19.

And the same is true of the transport squads. Had I, as you write, admitted 'the truth' *back then* in three-fourths crazy Berlin, neither Ebert, Noske or Lüttwitz, etc. would have been particularly happy. On the contrary, we took every precaution before the trial so that not a hair could be touched on anyone who had acted according to my orders on the night in question. Due to Captain Petri's interference by bribing Runge and the fact that this caused Vogel to lose his head, the court could not afford to acquit those two. Please do not forget as well that no one, neither the judge appointed by the Kav. Div. [GKSD] (General Freiherr v. Lüttwitz) nor his superior and commander-in-chief, Noske, made use of their right to reject the verdict of the division's court martial!

You clearly grasped the role played by lead negotiator Kriegsgerichts[rat] Erhard. My dear Herr Ertel, I cannot answer the question of the name of the regiment commander who approached the Div. Kdo. [division commander] with the curious wish to allow Frau Luxemburg to address his officers and NCOs. Many members of his family are still alive, and they would view it as an unfriendly gesture to publicly reveal what a dunderhead bore their name in those fateful years. It would be better to omit this episode, which I will not include in my gradually expanding memoirs for the same reason.

And now an observation in closing! I rather wonder that you, whom I consider a smart and experienced senior television worker, did not discover the links between the People's Deputies and the division long ago. Why else was this division dispatched to Berlin first, as the most reliable and best-led unit of the collapsing army (see page 36 of the *Generalstabswerk* about the battles in Berlin)[14] and why was it the only field division to remain mobile?? (page 47)

Don't you believe that, alongside an iron will, absolute secrecy does not also belong to the leadership of a squad with such a mission, which, as you write, it maintained for fifty years?

With best regards, also from my wife
Yours (W. Pabst)

---

14   Here he is referring to *Die Wirren*, see n. 7 <cl>.

Document VI: Draft of a Letter from Waldemar Pabst to Dr Heinrich Seewald[15]

Confidential

Dear Herr Seewald,

We have been through some highly turbulent weeks. Thanks to the energetic and most forceful intervention by the Düsseld[orf] police, the marches in 'honour' of the Communist leaders Liebkn[echt] a[nd] Luxemburg went off a lot more harmlessly than expected, following the propaganda employed a[nd] after the journalistic barrage (the latter reaching into the 'so-called bourgeois people'). Other than a [insertion: particularly] large shattered windowpane [insertion in pencil: several fireworks?] no damage was caused.[16]

On the advice of the local police, my wife and I removed ourselves from all 'ovations' for a little over a week and went on vacation to a lovely forest hotel; incidentally, we had numerous invitations from strangers far and wide to take a vacation at their homes, and after the broadcast on Südfunk Stuttgart came piles of letters a[nd] telegrams that

---

15   Source: BA-MA N 620/17, handwritten draft by Pabst of a letter (February or March 1969) to publisher Heinrich Seewald, Seewald-Verlag Stuttgart, who was to publish Pabst's memoirs. Pabst used a standard thank-you note from his eighty-eighth birthday on 24 December 1968 as rough paper.

16   Demonstrations took place in front of Pabst's house on 15 January 1969. Some demonstrators carried posters with Pabst's wanted poster. In Pabst's papers, BA-MA, N 620/21, a report from the Düsseldorf police dated 16 January 1969 lists the names and addresses of 15 participants!

I shall never find the time to answer. Particularly valuable is a letter from Martini.[17] Whether the mood will calm down cannot yet be predicted. Of the incoming letters roughly 9 in 10 support my decision at the time, [insertion: barely] 1/10 are of another opinion. Including several death threats.

Obviously, the last weeks have completely interrupted the progress of my memoirs, especially as my health is anything but satisfactory (heart specialist, had him for years already), the top doctor of the neurological institute and the top doctor of the eye clinic [insertion: as well as] my constant pharmaceutical needs are gradually swallowing significant portions of my fortune. And now lawyer fees will probably be incurred, from the suit launched by Souchon against Südfunk and the countersuit by the latter. All this belongs in the chapter 'Thanks to the Fatherland'. Back then, meaning January to March '19, the 'true citizens' could not, in terms of speed [a]nd quantity, call for us soldiers fast enough, I almost want to say on their knees, a[nd] now?? It was already a disgrace at the time that this trial took place, which neither Ebert nor Noske wanted. Noske had indeed promised [insertion: me] that it would not come to that, but the pressure from the [insertion: centre and] left wing of the S.P.D. was too great. My brave subordinates who volunteered for the deed were prosecuted rather than supported. No one dared to touch me, as 50,000 soldiers (Garde Kav[allerie] (Schü[tzen]) Div[ision] and Freikorps

---

17 Winfried Martini, a Munich-based publisher, had compared Luxemburg and Liebknecht to Hitler in the newspaper *Christ und Welt* 25, 22 June 1962, justifying their murder as the 'prophylactic murder of a tyrant'.

were then under the command of Gen[eral] v[on] Hofmann under the name G.[arde] Kav.[allerie] (Schü.[tzen]) Korps, had we deployed it would have been the end of the magnificence [insertion in pencil: not only of the Communists but also] of Weimar. Noske knew that I was prepared to do this [insertion: I told him so often enough, with him as commander-in-chief],[18] probably Ebert as well (not Hindenburg or Groener).

[Diagonally struck through] I would like to ask for your verbal advice as to what I should do if H.[er]r Souchon, who obstinately maintains that not he but Vogel fired the shot, does not calm down. The Südfunk's claim that he did it is a lie.

I of course did not personally lead or accompany the transports, I had more than enough to do that [insertion: January] night, which was pitch black, not even the street lights were back in operation everywhere.

I gave Souchon the order to eliminate Rosa, but he claims not to have carried it out, indeed, that he never received it!!! But he did see the shot being fired by transport leader Vogel, whom my Ib (now deceased)[19] had appointed transport leader as my proxy (Vogel did not belong to the division at all, he was stationed in the Hotel Eden as the underling of the western Einwohnerwehren [home guard]). [End of strikethrough]

You will easily gather from these lines why I was never pursued in court by the old S.P.D., just as Canaris, etc.

---

18   On this, see Bauer's estate in BA-Koblenz, N 1022/29, 8–10; Pabst's estate, BA-SAPMO, NY 4035/2, 17; Erger, *Der Kapp-Lüttwitz-Putsch*, 35ff; and Wette, *Noske*, 477ff and 506ff.

19   Second general staff officer Captain Heinz von Pflugk-Harttung.

never had difficulties (Ca.[naris] even became Noske's adjutant after getting Vogel to Holland).

Were I to open my mouth now after remaining silent for 50 years, it would cause considerable trouble. Perhaps devastating for the SPD in this election year?[20] on which I place no value, unless ... My idea was to reveal the hitherto unknown threads [insertion: and much more] in my memoirs.

But I will still manage to finish them, not least for financial reasons.

I would be most grateful for a prompt response, and hope to see you again soon, I am unfortunately incapable of travel, but you are in great shape to do so, and I can imagine that this trip would be valuable for your publishing house. Many heartfelt greetings from house to house always [end]

---

20   This assessment was perhaps exaggerated.

Document VII: Letter from the Lawyer Max Bürger to Waldemar Pabst, 4 February 1969[21]

Max Bürger I
Lawyer and Tax Law Specialist
4 Düsseldorf 1,
PO Box 2014

Herr
Dir. W. Pabst
4) Düsseldorf
Windscheidstr. 19

Excellency,

I tried to call you on Sunday evening several times. The first time I was connected. I introduced myself by name repeatedly, but then the receiver was hung up. My attempts at reconnection proved fruitless.

This afternoon I tried to get a connection to you again, from the office. This attempt was also in vain.

If you have not heard from me in these last two weeks it is because I have been, as it were, only 50% operational. The other 50% was taken by the flu. It is only very gradually improving.

From Stuttgart I have not, of course, heard anything new. I had hoped that the matter would peter out, but the broadcaster obviously does not want this, as a deadline for

---

21   Max Bürger was Waldemar Pabst's lawyer in 1919 and himself a member of the Garde-Kavallerie-Schützen-Division.

filing the suit in the main proceedings can only occur at the broadcaster's insistence.[22] The broadcaster is thus forcing Herr S.[ouchon] to file this suit. I tried to suggest that we should leave things in their present state. I had the impression that my attempt met with no success. The driving force is thus contrary to Herr Ertel's information the broadcaster.

My Stuttgart colleague[23] asked me to direct the following questions to you, the answering of which is a matter of discretion, that is, you must decide whether you wish to answer or not. The questions are:

1.) Did you give Herr S.[ouchon] any orders whatsoever? [handwritten note by Pabst:] to my knowledge, yes.

2.) Did Herr S.[ouchon] carry out these orders? [handwritten note by Pabst:] that's how it was reported to me by my deputy

3.) Upon what facts are the accusations against Herr S.[ouchon] based? [handwritten note by Pabst:] the Stuttgart colleague must ask Herr Ertel

4.) How did you become aware of this, since you were not present during the deed? [handwritten note by Pabst:] see no. 2.

5.) Did Herr S.[ouchon] inform you of the order being carried out? [handwritten note by Pabst] see no. 2.

I do not think it appropriate to handle these matters by

---

22 This refers to Souchon's provisional injunction forbidding Süddeutscher Rundfunk from broadcasting the docu-drama in which he was portrayed as the shooter. The programme was approved for broadcast with a preliminary disclaimer, however, on 14 and 15 January 1969 (see chapter fifteen).

23 This most likely refers to the lawyer Adolf Karch, who (on Otto Kranzbühler's recommendation) served as Souchon's authorized legal representative in Stuttgart.

telephone or through a written response. This should only be done verbally. As letters have already played a nefarious role in the Stuttgart proceedings, I beg you to destroy this letter.

Most sincerely,
Your most loyal
(Max Bürger)

Document VIII: Letter from Otto Kranzbühler
to Klaus Gietinger, 12 January 1993

Otto Kranzbühler, Lawyer
Tegernsee, 12.1.1993

Herr Klaus Gietinger
Frankfurt

Dear Klaus Gietinger,

Thank you very much for sending your work on clarifying the circumstances in which Rosa Luxemburg met her death. I read your investigation with interest and can only acknowledge the meticulousness of your research.

You will hardly be surprised if I nevertheless, and conclusively, remain of the opinion that Souchon was not the assassin. Without going into specifics, the following circumstances strike me as worth mentioning.

You are brave enough to declare as the perpetrator the man who always denied as much, namely Souchon,[24] and to declare the man who repeatedly identified himself as the perpetrator and was also identified as such in Souchon's testimony, namely Vogel, to not be the perpetrator.[25]

---

24   On Hermann W. Souchon's trustworthiness, see his false testimony given on 29 March 1919, his perjury in the trial itself on 9 May 1919, and his untrue statements in 1919, 1925 and 1968, claiming that he had stood in front of Pabst's room with his fellow soldiers, whereas they recall being inside and conspiring. (See chapter fifteen.)

25   Safely in Holland, Kurt Vogel would often claim to have shot Frau Luxemburg. However, this occurred at a time and in circles in which, to put it bluntly, it was 'fashionable' to brag about 'executing' the leader of the

Such a judgement against the testimony of the two persons most directly involved certainly requires overwhelming evidence to be convincing. Your finding, 'with a probability bordering on high certainty', that Souchon jumped onto the footboard and shot Rosa Luxemburg, and that it is 'highly unlikely' that the nervous Vogel fired before Souchon, will not convince any judge in light of the two participants' testimony. For me, the most important fact is one that is not adequately considered by your investigation. The vehicle in which Rosa Luxemburg was driven off [was] a six-seater Phaeton. According to his own testimony, Souchon sat on the right side in the middle row, behind the driver and in front of the row in which Rosa Luxemburg sat between the guards. In your depiction I can find no other passenger claiming this seat. It is equally certain that, because the vehicle was overfilled, it could not have been empty.

For me personally, another telling detail from Souchon is relevant, that he could only force himself into this seat with great effort given his imposing build, and that finding room for his carbine cost him additional effort.

This brings me to a further fact which you have overlooked. The naval officers were wearing military uniforms[26] and carrying carbines. Rosa Luxemburg, however, was

---

Communists, Rosa Luxemburg. Many did so. Vogel's penchant for showing off, however, went further – he claimed to have shot not only Luxemburg, but Liebknecht as well. He was blackmailing Pabst at the same time, threatening to tell the truth if not granted financial support.

26   I never denied that Souchon wore a soldier's uniform – on the contrary, I highlighted something curious: if he was wearing a soldier's uniform, then he was not serving as an officer, and thus was not recognized as one.

indisputably shot with a pistol.[27] The significance of this circumstance is not even mentioned in your paper.

I do not wish to go into further specifics, but rather to make two general points.

Firstly, your depiction lacks any explanation of the political situation of the day for today's reader, a necessity i[n] m[y] o[pinion]. A civil war was raging in Berlin – I experienced it myself as a twelve-year-old – and the choice was between Social Democracy or Communism of the Russian variety. Rosa Luxemburg had clearly articulated what to expect from this second current in 1909, with the demand that 'all who think and act differently must be shot without delay'. The praxis of Communism has confirmed this maxim entirely.

Only in light of this background can the Social Democratic government's participation and shared responsibility, for me unquestionable, be understood. Pabst assured me, as you know, that he called Noske before taking his decision. The latter first told him to obtain permission from General von Lüttwitz to execute the two prisoners, and following Pabst's reply, that he would never get it, responded with the words 'Then you must bear the responsibility for what has to be done'.[28]

Your definition of this as an officers' plot is i[n] m[y] o[pinion] historically incorrect.

---

27   No witness mentions a carbine rifle. Rosa Luxemburg's corpse exhibited an entry wound roughly 7mm in size (BA-MA, PH 8V/6, 19R). The soldiers in Pflugk-Harttung's unit, including Souchon, carried Mauser pistols, 7.65mm calibre. Vogel's weapon, a Luger (according to Souchon's 1925 testimony), was a 9mm calibre.

28   See chapter sixteen.

In closing, I would like to point to a sentence which particularly impressed me, albeit in the negative. According to your version, Pabst knew 'the naval officers would combine two things: an extraordinary training in killing and a fanatical hatred of Luxemburg and Liebknecht'. Pabst never said this.[29] You thus ascribe to him an opinion which can only be your own. As far as hatred is concerned, this is an emotion whose presence is problematic for an outsider. For an author writing about it after almost half a century,[30] it is, to put it mildly, totally unscientific.

As for the other part of your opinion, that naval officers had an extraordinary training in killing, I can, as a knowledgeable expert in this training, only shake my head. The focus of a naval officer's education was on piloting ships and using the weapons found on them, namely artillery, torpedoes and mines. Hand-to-hand combat, which you seem to view as training in killing, was not within the scope of this educational objective and for this reason did not take place.[31]

I deeply regret that you should have devalued your highly diligent, and in some respects insightful, work with such an unqualified personal opinion.

Sincerely
(Otto Kranzbühler)

---

29 Pabst remarked on this: 'if you want to classify Souchon within a particular group of people, there is only one word for it: he was a fanatic, but then so was I and my people', see document V, p.191.

30 He surely meant 'three-quarters'.

31 In *Wirren*, 53, it is affirmed that the volunteer officers' associations had 'contributed a great deal of good; they were mostly deployed as shock troops. … The regiment commander to whom such a department is subordinated during the fighting can be certain that every order will be carried out.'